THE BEHAVIOR OF GLASS AND OTHER MATERIALS EXPOSED TO FIRE

Edited by
Paul R. DeCicco, P.E.

Volume I
Applied Fire Science in Transition Series
Paul R. DeCicco: Series Editor

BAYWOOD PUBLISHING COMPANY, INC.
Amityville, New York

Library of Congress Catalog Number: 00-041428
ISBN: 0-89503-221-X (Paper)

Library of Congress Cataloging-in-Publication Data

The behavior of glass and other materials exposed to fire / edited by Paul R. DeCicco.
    p. cm. - - (Applied fire science in transition series ; v. 1)
    Includes bibliographical references and index.
    ISBN 0-89503-221-X (paper)
    1. Glass- -Fire testing. 2. Plastics- -Flammability. 3. Building materials- -Fire testing. I. DeCicco, Paul R., 1924- II. Series.

TH9446.5.G55 B45 2000
628.9'222- -dc21
    00-041428

Contents

INTRODUCTION

Volume I — The Behavior of Glass and Other Materials Exposed to Fire

Knowledge of the behavior of materials which, exposed to elevated temperatures, direct the course and consequences of structural fires is critical to the design of fire safe structures. Understanding how materials behave as fuel sources, as structural load bearing elements and as partitions which can resist penetration by heat, flames, smoke, and toxic gases is fundamental in every application of fire science. In this collection, a number of issues which have been of wide interest in recent years are addressed. They include: the behavior of glass exposed to fire stresses, the role of wood char in combustion, and the somewhat unexpected behavior of high strength concrete at elevated temperatures.

The time and modes of glass failure affect fire ventilation which in turn often controls fire development and growth and the advent of flashover and back draft phenomena. Char oxidation in certain fire environments also plays an important part in the overall production of heat energy and smoke during fires which threaten life safety. The behavior of such common building construction materials as high strength reinforced concrete and polymeric insulation materials whose use is expanding significantly, demands continued research and dissemination of guidelines and standards for their use.

In this volume, chapters by Hassani, Shields, and Silcock review the current level of knowledge regarding prediction of when glazing may be expected to fail under fire conditions, and present data from half-scale room experiments directed to the study of thermal strains in glazing exposed to an enclosure fire. The authors discuss test methodology and draw conclusions with respect to glazing exposed to non-uniform thermal environments in both single and double pane window glazing systems.

Chapters by Belles discuss flammability behavior of foam plastic insulation in garage doors as determined by an updated, room/corner test. Smoke and heat release measurements are used to judge product acceptance. Belles also presents information on chemically treated loose-fill cellulosic insulation and its behavior over time. He discusses fire experience, model code requirements, tendencies

1

toward smoldering and flaming propagation, and experience with fire retardant treatments. To complement some of the work by Hassani, Shields, and Silcock, Belles presents a chapter on the history of wired glass in fire rated applications. Here the author discusses the use of twenty-minute glazing in one-hour corridor partitions and identifies some of the issues associated therewith.

In a chapter by Yuen, Lo, and Yeoh the authors discuss protection of compartment wall openings through use of a double shutter fire door system in place of lobby enclosures. The separation and emissivity of the shutters are the key factors considered in establishing the effectiveness of the system. A computational Fluid Dynamics technique is used to analyze the influences of the two parameters.

The spalling of high strength concrete at elevated temperatures as presented by Ali, Connolly, and Sullivan examines the factors which contribute to spalling at elevated temperatures and notes that explosive spalling is exacerbated as the strength of the concrete increases. The authors describe other factors that contribute to the tendency for the concrete to spall and review measures for the prevention of spalling as reported by others.

Moghtaderi, Novozhilov, Fletcher, and Kent present the results of their study of the role of char oxidation on the flaming combustion characteristics of wood-based materials using a cone calorimeter. The work was done in order to produce more realistic models of wood combustion for use in a Computational Fluid Dynamics Model of building fires. The authors found that char oxidation is relatively important in the case of vertical orientation of the fire site amounting to 10 percent of the heat release.

Zhang, Shields, Silcock, and Azhakesan present the results of their work on the behavior of plywood lining in full scale room tests. Observations included ignition behavior, surface flame spread, and charring of the lining. The authors report different effects in three distinctly different regions of the corner tests performed. They describe experimental conditions and discuss the contribution of plywood to enclosure fires.

CHAPTER 1

An Experimental Investigation into the Behaviour of Glazing in Enclosure Fire

S. K. S. Hassani, T. J. Shields, and G. W. H. Silcock

Data from half scale room fire experiments are presented in which the thermal response of the enclosure with respect to the type of wall insulation and glazing employed are explored. Ceiling to floor fire gas temperature profiles, glass surface temperatures, time to first crack and crack bifurcation patterns are given. A report is made on the results of a preliminary experimental work dealing with the in-situ measurement of thermal strains in a glazing exposed to a real enclosure fire. The effect of a two layer environment in the fire enclosure on the performance of glazing is also addressed.

In several of the fire safety engineering calculations concerned with the growth and development of room fires it is assumed that the glazing system will completely and instantaneously fail when the upper gas layer temperature exceeds 500°C. Investigations on the behavior of glazing during enclosure fires has shown that the temperature differential and the resulting thermal expansion mismatch between the shaded and unshaded part of the glass is responsible for the glass breaking [1-3].

Analysis conducted on the performance of glazing systems subjected to room fires have utilized heat conduction equations to determine the temperature field in the glass. Joshi and Pagni [1] and Keski-Rahkonen [2], have independently developed mathematical models that predict the temperature field and the induced thermal stresses in the glass pane. However, in all these models oversimplifications have been made in the formulation of the problem and in the relevant boundary conditions to enable mathematical solutions. It was considered necessary therefore to conduct experimental studies to evaluate the validity of the predictions of such mathematical models.

3

In this chapter results of two separate sets of experiments are reported. In the first part, the data from half scale room fire experiments are presented whereby the thermal response of the enclosure with respect to the type of wall insulation and glazing employed are explored. Results indicate ceiling to floor fire gas temperature profiles, glass surface temperatures, time to first crack and, crack bifurcation patterns. The second part (see pages 15 and 17) reports on the results of experimental work concerned with the measurement of thermal strain in a glazing element exposed to an enclosure fire.

HALF-SCALE ROOM FIRE EXPERIMENTS

Experimental Details

A half scale experimental fire enclosure 1705 mm × 1525 mm × 1180 mm high was constructed as illustrated in Figure 1a. Three walls of the enclosure were built of 100 mm concrete blocks and insulated to form various types of construction, see Figure 2. The remaining façade of the enclosure was left open for the inclusion of a window frame and glazing unit. An air ventilation opening of dimensions 115 mm × 910 mm with movable slats was included at the rear of the right wall of the compartment. The ceiling was constructed of 6 mm "superlux" insulating board, with four 113 mm × 38 mm softwood joists with insulation quilt between them. The floor consisted of concrete blocks covered with an insulation quilt and superlux board. This provides a test facility that possesses similar heat and ventilation loss attributed to that of a typical domestic dwelling.

The fire load was selected according to the recommendation in Dingyi, i.e., the amount of fuel being proportional to the floor area [4]. As the floor in the half-scale compartment is equivalent to a quarter of the floor area in the full scale enclosure, and since a fire load density of 20 kg/m^2 represents the fire loading in a typical living-room environment, thus for the purpose of these half-scale tests a fire load density of 5 kg/m^2 was employed. This scaling was reflected in the use of wooden cribs 500 mm × 500 mm × 270 mm consisting of nine layers of nine sticks each measuring 30 mm × 30 mm × 500 mm, with a stick width to spacing ratio of 1:1.

The ambient ventilation rate for the enclosure was estimated using a tracer gas technique and found to be approximately six air changes per hour for an ambient temperature difference of 10°C which represents a rate typical of a room with the door partially open.

The glazing units employed for the various test scenarios each measured 905 mm × 1615 mm and were located in softwood frames 988 mm × 1690 mm. These included:

- single glazing (4 mm)
- single glazing (6 mm)
- double glazing (6 mm × 6 mm × 6 mm)
- low-emissivity double glazing (6 mm × 6 mm × 6 mm)

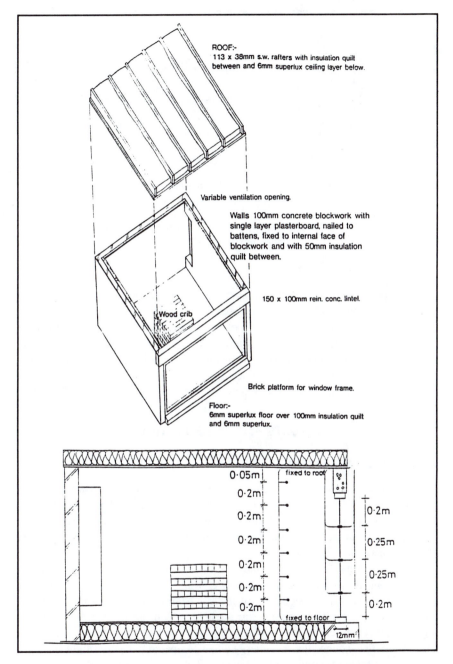

ROOF:-
113 x 38mm s.w. rafters with insulation quilt
between and 6mm superlux ceiling layer below.

Variable ventilation opening.

Walls 100mm concrete blockwork with
single layer plasterboard, nailed to
battens, fixed to internal face of
blockwork and with 50mm insulation
quilt between.

150 x 100mm rein. conc. lintel.

Wood crib

Brick platform for window frame.

Floor:-
6mm superlux floor over 100mm insulation quilt
and 6mm superlux.

0·05m   fixed to roof
0·2m
0·2m   0·2m
0·2m
0·2m   0·25m
0·2m
0·2m   0·25m
0·2m
0·2m   0·2m
            fixed to floor
                    12mm

Figure 1. (a) Half scale experimental compartment. (b) Section through
experimental compartment showing the position of thermocouples.

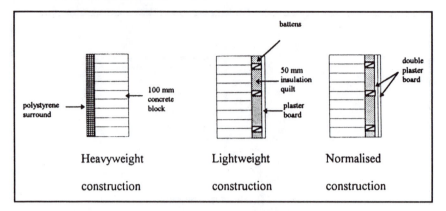

Figure 2. Different types of wall construction forming
half scale fire enclosure.

The experimental rig and the glazing units were instrumented as detailed in Figure 1b. Thermocouples were positioned on the surfaces of the glass to measure the glass surface temperatures. A tree of type K thermocouples was located near the inner glass surface to measure the floor to ceiling gas temperature profile. Strain gauges with copper-nickel foil material on a polyamide base were positioned in the shaded region of the inner pane of a double glazing unit, on the fire side to measure the development of thermally induced edge strains, see Figure 3.

RESULTS AND OBSERVATIONS

Gas Temperature Profile

Three types of enclosure wall structures were examined and for each construction type four different glazing units were employed. The gas temperature variation with height for each of the fire enclosures are shown in Figures 4-6. The individual curves which represent a single fire test can be partitioned into three distinct zones.

Variations in the fire gas temperature at twenty minutes over the height of the enclosure are shown to be as high as 400°C from floor to ceiling, with the upper gas temperatures exceeding 500°C. It is clear from the examination of Figure 5 that the highest gas temperatures are attained within the hot gas layer for the lightweight construction. This is due to the fact that low thermal inertia of walls absorb less fire induced thermal energy when compared to heavyweight structure which has a higher thermal inertia shown in Figure 4. It has been shown that the lightweight structure can, when necessary, be modified to give thermal response similar to that of a heavyweight structure for up to twenty after start of the fire by

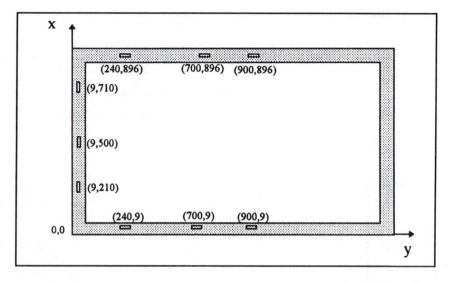

Figure 3. Position of strain gauges in the shaded area of the glass.

increasing the thickness of the inner plaster layer. This response is depicted in Figure 6 for a normalized structure. A wall construction of this type will have a lower "U" value (steady state thermal transmittance) than a lightweight structure and a similar transient thermal response to that of the heavyweight structure.

The significance of the results, however, is that in a typical room fire the vertical gas temperature profile is not uniform for a considerable time and there exists a large temperature variation from ceiling to floor. Hence a large window extending from floor to ceiling level will be exposed simultaneously to the upper hot gases and to the lower cooler gases.

Glass Surface Temperature Profile

Due to non-uniformity in the gas temperature profile over the enclosure height, the temperature attained in the pane of glass is also expected to be non-uniform in both exposed and shaded regions. To investigate this, thermocouples making good mechanical point contact were positioned on the inner glass surface of a double glazing unit in three different positions with respect to height, in both the shaded and unshaded regions, see inset in Figure 7. For the glazing unit incorporated in a heavyweight fire enclosure the temperature profiles are given in Figure 7 which includes also the time at which the first crack occurred. At 7.5 minutes from the initiation of the fire (the time at which the first crack occurred at the top edge of the glass) the top thermocouple in the exposed region of the glass indicated a temperature around 230°C whereas the other lower placed thermocouples on the exposed region of the glass did not indicate any substantial increase from the

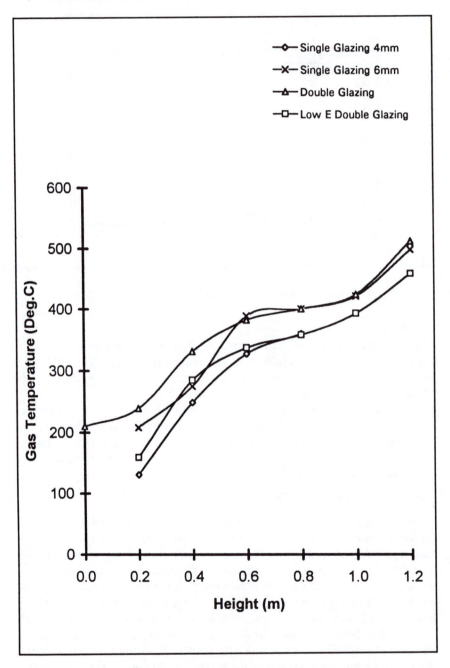

Figure 4. Gas temperature profile over the height of fire enclosure at twenty minutes from ignition time (heavyweight construction).

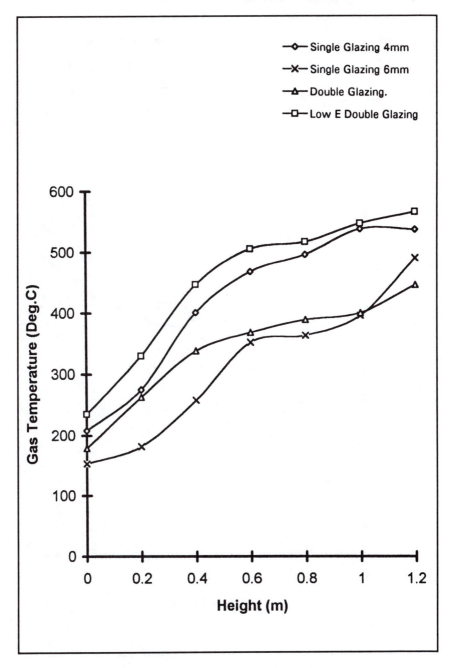

Figure 5. Gas temperature profile over the height of fire enclosure at twenty minutes from ignition time (lightweight construction).

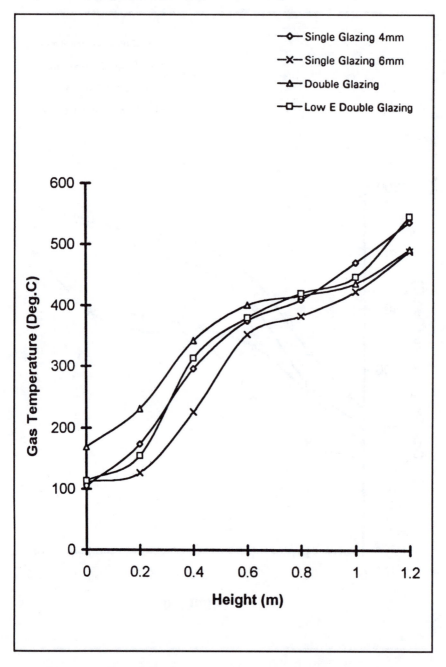

Figure 6. Gas temperature profile over the height of fire enclosure at twenty minutes from ignition time (normalized construction).

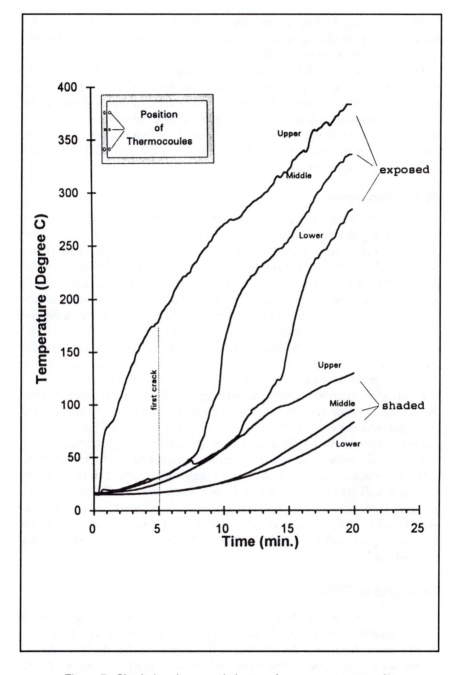

Figure 7. Shaded and exposed glass surface temperature profile over the height for fire enclosure with heavyweight structure.

initial temperature. Also the thermocouples in the shaded regions of the glass did not indicate any significant increase in the temperature above ambient during this period. Therefore, it can be seen that the surface temperatures of the pane of glass in the exposed region follow the enclosure fire gas temperature profile. It should be noted that the mathematical models dealing with breakage of glass assume that glass is subjected to a uniform heating environment [1, 2]. In these models the average temperature at the center of the pane of glass is taken as a reference temperature regarding the criterion for cracking, assuming that the shaded edge remains at its initial temperature. Clearly this is not the case for large picture windows as demonstrated above.

Glazing Performance

The crack initiation sites and the crack bifurcation patterns suffered by glazing systems during the various fire tests are shown in Figure 8 and Figure 9 for lightweight and normalized structures respectively. The crack initiations are numbered according to the order of occurrence with the first crack numbered 1, second crack numbered 2, etc. The first crack invariably occurs in the edge contained in the top section where it heats up first. All the crack initiation sites and the subsequent bifurcation routes occur in the upper half of the glazing during the first twenty minutes which reflects the effect of a two zone heating environment in the fire enclosure. During this period the cracks in the glass did not join to form areas enclosed by a continuous bifurcation route and therefore were incapable of falling out, except in the case of 6 mm single glazing located in lightweight structure where approximately 50 percent of the glass pane fell out at fifteen minutes from the fire initiation and the 6 mm single glazing in the normalized structure. In the latter case however, the section of glazing marked by continuous bifurcation routes remained in situ for the remainder of the test which suggests that the formation of a continuous bifurcation route is not the only condition for glass fall out.

The performance during fire of glazing systems incorporated in an enclosure of various wall structures is given in Table 1 where time for first crack, upper gas layer temperature at that time, shaded and exposed glass surface temperatures measured at the top section, difference in temperature between shaded and unshaded regions and, the amount of glass remaining in-situ at twenty minutes are tabulated.

Comments on Table

In all cases the time for first crack was found to occur in the range seven to thirteen minutes from the time of fire initiation. In the case of double glazing units the first crack occurred in the top edge of the inner pane. For the low e double glazing systems the time to first crack and the subsequent bifurcation patterns were similar to ordinary double glazing units, and also similar to those for 4 mm and 6 mm single glazing units. All the window units retained integrity for over

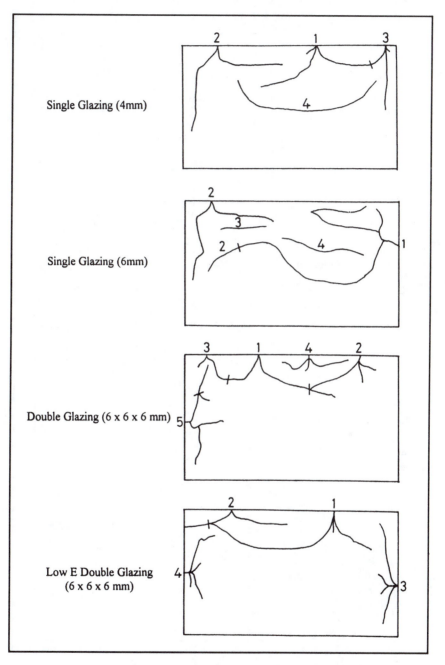

Single Glazing (4mm)

Single Glazing (6mm)

Double Glazing (6 x 6 x 6 mm)

Low E Double Glazing
(6 x 6 x 6 mm)

Figure 8. Crack initiation sites and crack patterns in various glazing
systems for lightweight room construction.

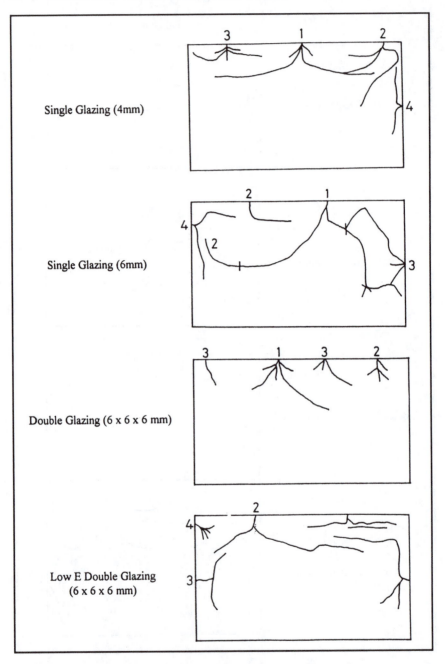

Single Glazing (4mm)

Single Glazing (6mm)

Double Glazing (6 x 6 x 6 mm)

Low E Double Glazing
(6 x 6 x 6 mm)

Figure 9. Crack initiation sites and crack patterns in various glazing systems for normalized room construction.

Table 1. Glazing Performance in a Fire Enclosure with High
Ventilation for Various Wall Structures

	Single Glazing 4 mm	Single Glazing 6 mm	Double Glazing 6 × 6 × 6 mm	Double Glazing Low E
Normalized Construction				
Time for first crack (mins., secs.)	8.45	10.43	7.10	13.00
Upper gas layer temperature at this time °C	345	389	347	346
Shaded/unshaded glass temperature °C	59/188	60/190	59/180	60/167
Temperature difference °C	129	130	121	107
Percent of pane remaining in-situ at twenty minutes	100%	100%	100%	100%
Heavyweight Construction				
Time for first crack (mins., secs.)	8.30	8.50	8.00	10.30
Upper gas layer temperature at this time °C	409	467	589	464
Shaded/unshaded glass temperature °C	79/226	74/219	81/232	73/220
Temperature difference °C	147	145	151	147
Percent of pane remaining in-situ at twenty minutes	100%	100%	100%	100%
Lightweight Construction				
Time for first crack (mins., secs.)	7.50	7.45	7.10	7.50
Upper gas layer temperature at this time °C	323	431	382	385
Shaded/unshaded glass temperature °C	44/169	49/195	46/176	51/179
Temperature difference °C	125	146	130	128
Percent of pane remaining in-situ at twenty minutes	100%	50%	100%	100%

twenty minutes except for the 6 mm single glass pane incorporated in a lightweight construction in which 50 percent of the glass fell out at fifteen minutes after the time of fire initiation. This event is illustrated in Figure 10 where the hot gas layer temperature profile is compared for various glazing systems in a lightweight room construction. The effect of new openings caused by loss of glass for the case mentioned previously is demonstrated by a sharp rise in the upper gas layer temperature to 800°C, an event usually associated with flash over.

EXPERIMENTAL DETERMINATION OF EDGE STRAINS

The work reported above indicates that in a two zone enclosure fire the initial fracture occurs in the top half of the glazing, and that these cracks do not

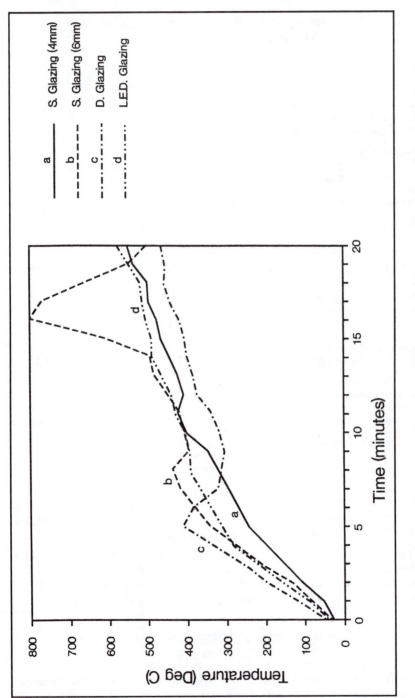

Figure 10. Hot gas layer temperature profile for various glazing systems in a lightweight room construction.

propagate into the lower half of the glazing. This suggests that the lower half of the pane of glass may be under a different state of stress. Thus it was decided to explore the state of this stress field along the edges of the window glass as the enclosure fire developed.

Experimental Methods and Details

A 38 mm wide wooden frame with an 18 mm wide glazing slip having a similar overall dimension as those reported earlier was constructed to house a double glazing unit with glass dimensions of 1615 mm × 905 mm × 6 mm and air gap of 8 mm was located in a heavyweight type enclosure. Strain gauges having a copper-nickel foil material on a polyamide base were placed in the shaded region of the inner pane and 9 mm from the edges in various positions as shown in Figure 3. The axis of the strain gauges were aligned parallel to the edges since it was noted that principal stress in the glass was in the direction parallel to the edges [5]. The output of these strain gauges with respect to time for the first ten minutes of the test is given in Figure 11.

Observation and Results

The positive strains indicate a state of tension and the negative strain values indicate a state of compression in the pane of glass (see Figure 11). The occurrence of a crack in the glass can be detected by marking the sudden relaxation in the level of stress. The experiment was also video taped to allow visual inspection. The time and position of first crack extracted from the video tape agreed with the results obtained from the strain versus time graphs.

The non-uniform heating of glass caused by the two zone enclosure fire is responsible for the development of a complex stress field in the glass (see Figure 11). This shows the stress developed in the upper and lower edge of the glass with respect to time during the first ten minute period. This clearly illustrates that a non-uniform stress is developing in the shaded region of the glass pane as the hot gas layer temperature in the half scale fire room rises. Along the top edge of the inner pane thermal strains increase with a similar rate for all the three locations shown, peaking to a value of 600 microstrain. Along the bottom edge of the inner pane thermal strains are negative indicating a state of compression for at least the first seven minutes.

Analysis of Results

Fracture faces were obtained from the fracture sites in the pane of the glass to enable the observation of the fracture mode and calculation of stress level at fracture, see Figure 12. The values obtained from strain gauges are supported by the calculations using an expression given by Orr for estimating the tensile stress σ (MPa) [6].

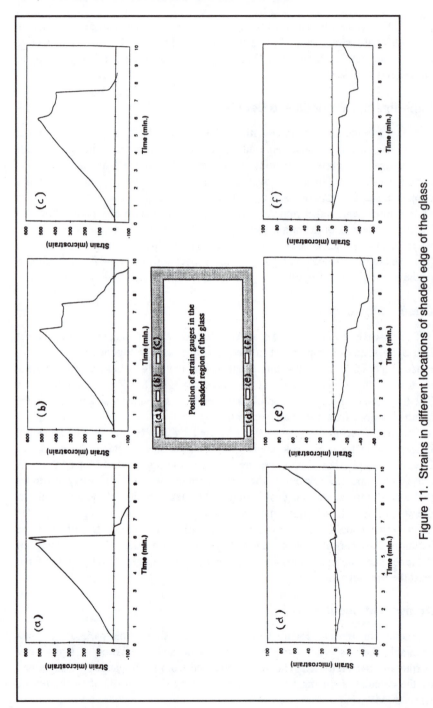

Figure 11. Strains in different locations of shaded edge of the glass.

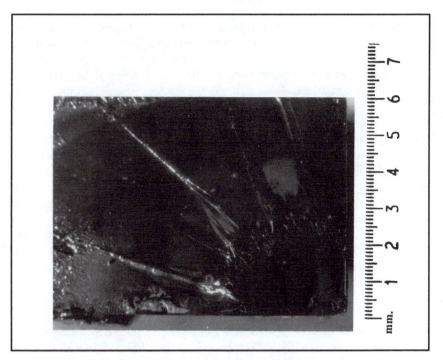

Figure 12. Fracture face from a crack in glass subjected to an enclosed fire, showing mirror, mist, and hacked regions. The mirror radius is ≃ 2.2 mm.

The tensile stress is estimated using

$$\sigma = 67.8 / \sqrt{r} \tag{1}$$

where r (mm) is the radius of the smooth mirror section of the fracture face. Such a fracture face is illustrated in Figure 12 which was taken from a crack at the top edge of the same glass pane for which strains were measured. The corresponding r value is found to be 2.2 mm which when incorporated into equation (1) yields a stress at fracture of 48 MPa. From strain measurements, the strain at fracture is shown to be approximately 550 microstrains. Using Hookes law, i.e.,

$$\sigma = E.\varepsilon \tag{2}$$

and assuming that Young's modulus E for glass is 80 GPa, a value of 44 MPa for tensile stress at fracture is obtained which agrees with the value calculated using equation (1).

At six minutes from the start of the fire, a fracture occurs in the vicinity of the left hand side strain gauge which causes the strain to relax, Figure 11a. The test was video taped and from a close inspection of the video it was concluded that the location and time of the fracture coincided with the strain gauge outputs. It was noted that the state of the stress in the bottom edge was totally different to that at the top edge during the same period as the bottom edge which was experiencing compression, Figure 11e. This explains why the bottom section of the glass did not crack until some considerable time later in the fire test. It was also observed that the crack initiated in the top edge did not propagate into the lower half of the glass pane. In situ measurement of the strain developing in the window glass indicates that a complex stress field is prevailing. A schematic view of the possible stress field in window glass at a point in time six minutes after the fire initiation is illustrated in Figure 13. This observation further supports the theoretical view that glass cracking can only occur in edges experiencing tension and is also in agreement with previous experimental observations. This suggests that if the stress field in the glass could be determined analytically it should be possible to predict preferred fracture bifurcation routes. Such a development would then enable the fire safety engineer to assess the likelihood and the extent of the glass fall out for a given fire scenario.

CONCLUSIONS

1. Thermal response of an enclosure can be altered if desired by simple and effective modifications to the wall construction, e.g., a lightweight wall structure can be modified by the addition of a layer of plaster to change its thermal response, when necessary, to resemble that of a heavyweight structure with a higher thermal inertia for the first twenty to thirty minutes of an enclosure fire.

2. An enclosure with medium to high ventilation could have a significantly large temperature gradient over its height for a considerable time during a fire. Hence, a tall window with a large pane of glass (typical in new buildings with large picture windows) incorporated in such an enclosure would experience a significant temperature gradient over its height.

3. The first crack in the window glass subjected to a two zone fire environment almost always occurs in the edges contained in the hot gas layer.

4. Crack bifurcations were contained only in the upper half of the pane of glass for a considerable time (in these experiments for up to 15 minutes). The crack branches did not readily join to form a continuous path which is considered to be the main but not the only prerequisite for glass fall out.

5. Contrary to the common belief that window glass falls out completely in early stages of an enclosure fire, even single glazing remained in-situ for a considerable time. In the case of double glazing units only some sections of the inner pane fell out after fifteen minutes from the start of fire, thereafter the outer pane only sustained some cracking.

6. The state of stress in the glass subjected to a non-uniform heating environment was shown to change over the height of the glass, with tensile stresses in the top edge and compressive stresses in the bottom edge of the glass.

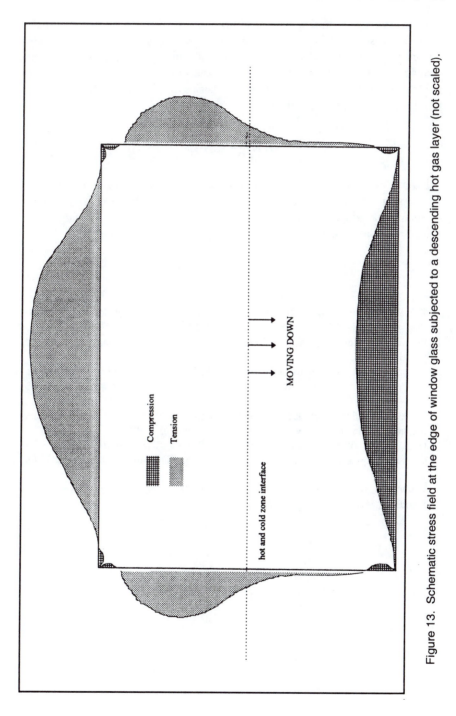

Figure 13. Schematic stress field at the edge of window glass subjected to a descending hot gas layer (not scaled).

7. Strain gauge technology can be utilized to evaluate the real in-situ thermally induced stresses in the pane of glass subjected to real enclosure fires. Stress values obtained by this method can be used for validation of mathematical models dealing with the breakage of glass in fire and ultimately as an input into fire models dealing with pre-flash over the post-flash over enclosure fire in the form of providing available ventilation opening.

FUTURE WORK

Further experiments involving multi-pane glazing systems are currently in progress in which edge strain in each pane will be determined. The analysis of such work will further contribute to a more complete understanding of the behavior of glazing in real enclosure fires.

REFERENCES

1. P. J. Pagni and A. A. Joshi, Glass Breaking in Fires, *Proceedings of Third International Symposium on Fire Safety Science,* pp. 791-802, 1991.
2. O. Keski-Rahkonen, Breaking of Glass Close to Fire, I, *Fire and Materials, 12,* pp. 61-69, 1988.
3. S. K. S. Hassani, J. S. Shields, and G. W. Silcock, Thermal Fracture of Window Glazing: Performance of Glazing in Fire, *Journal of Applied Fire Science, 4*:4, pp. 249-263, 1994-95.
4. H. Dingyi, Evaluation of Quarter-scale Compartment Fire Modelling for Constant and Stepped Heat Inputs, *Fire and Materials, 11,* pp. 179-190, 1987.
5. G. E. Blight, Thermal Strain and Fracture of Building Glass, *First Australian Conference on Engineering Materials,* NSW University, New South Wales, pp. 685-700, 1974.
6. L. Orr, Practical Analysis of Fractures in Glass Windows, Materials Research and Standards, *MTRSA, 12*:1, pp. 21-47, 1972.

CHAPTER 2

Thermal Fracture of Window Glazing: Performance of Glazing in Fire

S. K. S. Hassani, T. J. Shields, and G. W. H. Silcock

Windows constituting part of compartment walls are important features in that they depict the maximum potential ventilation opening factor should the glazing fail as the result of a fire. In the development of fire safety engineering solutions, it is necessary to be able to accurately predict the behavior of glazing systems subjected to different thermal fields. This chapter reviews the current level of knowledge gained through analytical and experimental work reported in literature relevant to this phenomenon. Limitations in the current knowledge base together with areas requiring future research are highlighted.

Most room enclosure fires are ventilation controlled, consequently, windows in an enclosure which depict the maximum potential ventilation opening, should the glazing fail in a fire, assume special significance. For the purpose of fire safety engineering calculations, it has been convenient to assume that given a fire, the glass instantaneously disintegrates, providing the maximum ventilation area. Although this assumption is accepted as a gross simplification of a complex process, it is necessary however, in the development of credible fire safety engineering solutions, to be able to accurately predict the behavior of window glass subjected to different fire scenarios.

The mechanism of glass breakage in windows as the result of thermally induced stresses is well understood [1-18]. When glass fixed in window framing is subjected to a thermal field, only the exposed area of glass is heated, i.e., the covered edge of the glass is shielded by the framing from incident radiative and convective heating. Glass is a poor conductor and hence heat from the area exposed to the thermal environment is not readily conducted to the edge region. In addition, the window framing may also act as a heat sink and contribute to keeping the shaded area of the glass at lower temperatures. Temperature differentials between the exposed and shaded regions of glass will induce differential thermal expansion in these regions. The thermal expansion of the heated area of glass is in turn constrained by the cooler edge region. Consequently the shaded region is placed in tension. Ultimately, when the edge tensile stresses reach a critical level, cracking occurs.

Defects such as notches, chipping, etc., in the edges of the glass caused by cutting and handling may result in high local stress concentrations. These defects aid the initiation of cracking at the edge of the glass, at stress levels (breaking stress, σ_b) lower than the glass tensile strength (determined by mechanical testing).

Over the past two decades, efforts have been made to determine the temperature fields and associated stress fields in glass subjected to thermal insult in order to predict when and how fracture occurs and propagates. This chapter reviews relevant published work [1-16] dealing with solar and fire induced thermal stress and relates it to the specific problem of window breaking in enclosure fires. The literature reviewed in this chapter is summarized in the appendix. Areas identified for new work essential for the advancement of the present level of knowledge and the development of fire engineering models are highlighted.

THERMAL AND STRESS FIELD EVALUATION

It has been established [1] that the cause of fracture in glazing when subjected to fire is the non-uniform heating of the glass which produces thermally induced stresses, leading to the initiation of cracking. Theoretically the breaking stress σ assumes the form "$\sigma \propto \Delta T(t)$," where $\Delta T(t)$ is a typical temperature difference between the shaded and unshaded region of the glass at time 't'.

The temperature distribution, $T(x,y,z,t)$ in pane of glass can be determined using:

- numerical thermal analysis [2, 3, 4, 10, 12]
- finite element analysis [9, 11]
- experimental techniques [6-8, 13]

Methods of numerical thermal analysis used to determine the temperature distribution in glass, employ one or two dimensional heat conduction equations which incorporate a separate radiation component [2] or alternatively a normalized conduction equation which includes a radiation contribution [3]. In Shelley, Roby, and Beyler, the theoretical models the imposed heat flux is assumed to be uniform across the exposed area of the glass. From the analytically or experimentally derived temperature distributions, the exposed glass temperature rise is approximated by either taking the average rise in surface temperature of both sides measured at the center [3], or a thickness averaged temperature rise at the center of the pane [2]. The temperature difference responsible for cracking may then be approximated to the exposed glass average temperature rise at the center since the edge is assumed to remain at its initial temperature.

The temperature difference in the shaded and unshaded region of glass ΔT is related to the induced stresses by the use of simple strain criterion [4, 5]. i.e.:

$$\Delta T = \frac{1}{d} \int_0^d T(x,t)dx - T_i = g\sigma_b/E\beta \tag{1}$$

where:

$T(x,t)$ = temperature as a function of glass thickness and time
T_i = initial temperature
g = force balance factor (=1.0)
E = elastic (Young's) modulus for glass ($\approx$80 GPa)
β = thermal expansion coefficient of glass ($\approx$80 $\times$ 10^{-6}/°C)
d = glass thickness
σ_b = breaking of the glass

This simply implies that the thickness-averaged temperature rise at the center of exposed glass over that at the shaded edge produces a thermal stress at the edge which exceeds the glass tensile strength. In [3] the temperature distribution is related to stress by Airy's stress function, i.e.:

$$\frac{d^2}{dz^2} (\sigma_y + \beta \cdot E \cdot T(z,t)) = 0 \tag{2}$$

where z is in a direction normal to the glass edge, Figure 1. Temperature across the glass thickness is assumed to be constant. However, it is noted that for most practical purposes where the built-in edge is much smaller than the glass pane dimensions, the edge stress can be conveniently approximated by the strain criterion given in equation (1).

Experimental studies [6, 7] have been carried out to validate these models. In [6] a fast fire was produced in a small experimental fire compartment which incorporated a window (28 cm $\times$ 50 cm) in the upper section of the compartment wall so that the entire glass pane was submerged in the hot gas layer within ten seconds. The results in this case were in good agreement with those predicted by the models. However, when large windows (i.e., the glazing extending from upper hot zone to lower cold zone of fire compartment) were used in a series of fifty half-scale fire room experiments [7], the behavior of glazing differed significantly from that predicted using the existing theoretical models. The lower section of glass did not fracture for a long time after the initiation of fire. The glass panes remained in-situ for some considerable time and when some part of glass did fall

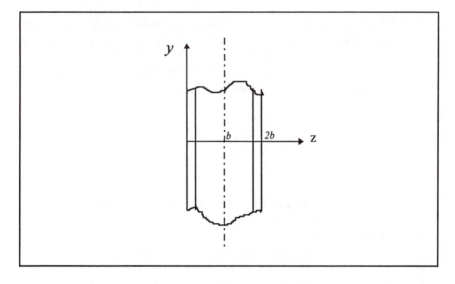

Figure 1. A long window strip of width 2b covered
at longitudinal edge [3].

out it occurred only from the upper section of the pane where bifurcated cracks
joined to form a network.

Studies on the performance of solar control glazing reported similar effects on
the framed glass panes [8-11]. The results and understanding gained from the
research work on the thermal breakage of solar control glazing are directly
relevant to the problem of glass breakage in fire since in both cases the underlying
cause of fracture is thermally induced stress. Here it was established that non-
uniform heating, not only due to edge cover by the frame but also due to shadows
on the exposed part of glass (e.g., from protruding building elements such as a
mullion or from an adjacent tree, etc.), had a marked effect on the stress field
development in the glass. This behavior is analogous to the non-uniform heating
of exposed glass due to the descending hot gas layer formed during an enclosure
fire that initially encompasses only the upper section of glass pane. In a slowly
developing enclosure fire the window glass can be subjected to a two zone heating
environment for a period long enough to influence the fracture behavior of the
glass. This effect and the resulting behavior of glazing has only been addressed in
[7] and currently in a research program at the University of Ulster concerned with
the breakage of glass subjected simultaneously to hot and cold fire gas zones.

As an integral part of the research program at University of Ulster the authors
have also carried out preliminary experiments [17] in which the edge stress in a
glass pane subjected to a two zone heating environment was measured in-situ. The
results suggest that window's geometry and location control the resulting thermal

stresses and as such affect the performance of glazing during an enclosure fire. It is abundantly clear from these experiments that the effect of descending hot gas layer on the performance of glazing in an enclosure fire requires further in depth study.

STRESS PATTERNS

It has been established that when window glass is subjected to a thermal field the stress created in the shaded edge is uniaxial tension parallel to the edge, while in the heated area in the vicinity of the edge, stress is uniaxial compression [8]. In the corner region of the glass stress approximates to an isotropic compression reducing to zero at the physical corner. Therefore, the most likely location for the initiation of cracks is along the edges at some distance from the corners. Glass edge quality can influence the stress at fracture since the existence of a notch or a chipping at the glass edge increases the stress concentration. The importance of edge defects can be best understood using fracture mechanics principles and demonstrated particularly by the Griffith's criterion, i.e.,

$$\varepsilon_t = const. \left(\frac{\gamma}{EC} \right)^{\frac{1}{2}} \tag{3}$$

where ε_t is strain at failure, E is Young's modulus, γ is the fracture surface energy of the glass and, C is the equivalent dimension of defect or flaw in the glass at the point of fracture initiation. Clearly, the better the condition of the edge, the smaller C will be and the greater will be the resultant strain capacity.

For the estimation of breaking stress of glass four point bend tests were carried out [14] and the results were treated by Weibull analysis to ascertain the glass breaking stress distribution. A breaking stress of 40 MPa was determined to be a reasonable estimate to use in breaking calculations for ordinary soda glass. However, a single strength value for glass with edges of differing quality resulting from different methods of glass cutting (e.g., hand cut, machine cut, and edge beveled, etc.) may not be sufficient. Perhaps the edge quality should be categorized as follows. "Excellent" for as machine cut, ground and beveled, "Good" for as machine cut only, and "Poor" for as hand cut. For each edge quality classification a factor may then be associated with the characteristic strength of glass used in computer models to predict more accurately the behavior of glass in end use conditions.

MULTIPANE GLAZING UNITS

Finite element studies were conducted on double glazed windows subjected to solar heating [11], in which it was shown that three dimensional effects across the thickness of the window are negligible, i.e., in-plane forces and bending moments are not transmitted in any significant way from one pane to another. However, it is necessary to be able to predict, in the case of the fire performance of windows with multiple glazing, the extent and the mode of heat transfer to the outer panes before and after the breaking of the first pane.

Using mathematical models the performance of double glazed windows in a wild fire were predicted [15]. It was suggested that the pane facing the fire would shield the second pane from the oncoming heat flux thereby keeping it cool. If the first pane were to fall out, the second pane would then begin to heat up and crack. The resulting behavior of the system is largely expected to depend on whether the first pane would fall out completely or partially. The results of experiments on the performance of double glazed units incorporating ordinary and low emissivity glass carried out at the University of Ulster [18] indicated that double glazing units could retain integrity in real fires for over thirty minutes. This finding is in contrast to the common perception that the glazing will probably disintegrate early in the development of fire. Thus the assumed ventilation opening may not be available which could result in a low energy fire with overtone of backdraught for fire fighters. Experimental investigation is required to determine whether a partially collapsed inner pane, for example, would affect the heat transfer to the outer pane, i.e., the temperature distribution and stress field in the outer pane.

In the preliminary experimental program at the University of Ulster [19] the temperature variations across and through *purpose* built double glazed units were measured using type K thermocouples which were attached to the exposed face, unexposed face and on the glass surfaces forming the air gap. From a preliminary analysis of these results it was concluded that the temperature profiles across the system and on the panes was non-uniform. Variations were noted between the treated (low emissivity) units and the normal untreated units. By definition low emissivity glazing transmits less energy from the room of fire origin. Hence this is expected to have an accelerating effect on the development of the fire growth given sufficient ventilation.

At the present a program of work is underway to determine the in-situ stresses at the unexposed edges for the treated and untreated double glazed systems under the thermal insult from a typical two zone enclosure fire.

CONCLUDING NOTES

1. The assumption that the window glazing in an enclosure fire is subjected to a uniform heat flux across the exposed section of the glass [2, 3, 5, 12, 16] can only be valid for a very fast fire in an enclosure incorporating a window placed in the upper hot zone section of the room.

2. It has been demonstrated that larger picture windows, i.e., floor to ceiling height, will be subjected to a two zone heating regime imposed by descending hot gas layer [7]. It is therefore necessary to investigate the dynamic development of the induced stress field experimentally for various descent rates of the hot gas layer which in turn is dictated by the nature of fire.

3. Cracks initiate at the edges since the maximum tensile stress occurs in the shaded region of the glass and that these edges contain locations of high stress concentration.

4. The quality of the edge of the glass will have a marked effect on the strain capacity of the glass [8, 14]. It is therefore suggested that further research is required to be carried out to relate the edge condition to the strain capacity of the glass.

5. Much of the research work to date has been conducted using single pane glazing systems which does not reflect the fact that there is more frequent use of double and multiple glazing in buildings. It is essential to conduct experimental investigations into the behavior of such glazing systems subjected to the thermal insult of an enclosure fire.

6. The assumption that window glass instantly disintegrate in real fire environments is grossly invalid.

7. Multi-pane glazing units retain their integrity in real fire for much longer than conventional wisdom suggests.

8. The behavior of multi-pane glazing units in a real fire could have significant beneficial impact on:

- cost effective fire engineering solutions, e.g., atrium building
- the design of smoke management systems
- external fire spread

9. The interaction between fire growth and multi-pane glazing units, especially Low Emissivity units, given adequate ventilation demands further investigation.

10. The results of work to investigate thermal breakage in the solar control glazing units could be usefully employed in fire safety engineering.

Appendix I.   Executive Summary of Reference Literature

No.	Author and Date	Type of Paper[a]	Executive Summary
1	Emmons, H. W. 1989	Review	Addresses those areas of fire engineering which has not been researched and those areas which need further attention. One of such areas thought of as important in the growth and development of enclosure fire was the breakage of window glass in an enclosure fire. This paper highlighted the need for scientific study on the behaviour of glazing in fire.
2	Joshi, A. A. Pagni, P. J. 1990	Analyt.[L]	Make use of transient, one dimensional (into the glass normal to the pane), inhomogeneous (in-depth radiation absorption) energy equation to **output**: — surface temperature history $T(0, \tau)$ of the glass — temperature at breaking, i.e., when $\{T(0,\tau) - T_i\} \cdot \alpha \cdot E = \sigma_b$ — suggest $\Delta T = 50°C - 100°C$ — results are presented for a set of varying parameters — in this work it is assumed uniform flux imposed on glass — no effective hot and cold zone in fire compartment is considered
3	O. Keski-Rahkonen 1988	Analyt.[L]	— uses two dimensional heat equation to get temperature and stress distribution in the glass subjected to fire. **Output:** • $\overline{T(x,\tau)}$ temperature profile in terms of x and time, assuming **dT/dL = 0** where L = thickness, **dT/dY = 0**, and **Bi < 0.1**, i.e., assume uniform heating of glass pane • $\sigma_y(x, \tau)$ – stress in y direction in terms of x and time • Suggests that distinction must be made between cracking and loss of integrity. For integrity two levels must be identified; 1. cracks at t_1 making fire spread through a barrier possible 2. breaking of glass pane at t_2 where large open areas of window (fall outs) allow gas flow

4	Joshi, A. A. Pagni, P. J. 1991	Computer Model

— instructions on use of BREAK computer programme.

Output:
describes temperature profile T(x,t) where x is distance into thickness

$$T(x,t) \text{ is inserted in } \Delta T = \frac{1}{L} \int_0^l T(x,t)\,dx - T_i = g\frac{\sigma_b}{E\beta} \text{ to calculate the time to glass breakage}$$

(g—geometry factor of order 1).

5	Pagni, P. J. Joshi, A. A. 1991	Analyt.[L]

— extends the analysis described in No. 2 above to obtain temperature profile and stress profile in terms of x,y and time, taking into account the effect of heat dissipation into the shaded area of the glass.

— assumption is made that glass is subjected to a uniform hot gas at the inner surface

6	Skelly, M. J. Roby, R. J. Beyler, C. L. 1991	Exp.[L]

— experimentally investigated the window glass breakage in enclosure fires
— fire compartment; 1.5 × 1.2 × 1.0m
— glass pane 0.28 × 0.5 × 0.024m
— fire source; liquid hexane
— window was placed in fire compartment in such a way that in all tests entire glass was in hot zone within 10 secs
— glass was cut by hand and edges were not prepared in any way

Output:
a. time-temperature profile for shaded and unshaded glass for various fire sizes
b. tabulated temperature difference with time of crack initiation
c. bifurcation patterns
d. compared experimental results with theoretical work of Pagni (ref. 2) and Keski-Rahkonen's (ref. 3).

Appendix I. (Cont'd.)

No.	Author and Date	Type of Paper[a]	Executive Summary
7	Silcock, G. W. Shields, T. J. 1993	Exp.[L]	— fire compartment; a half scale fire room — single and double glazing with wooden frame — fire source; wooden cribs **Output:** a. time to first crack b. shaded/unshaded temperature difference c. crack bifurcation patterns d. effect of two zone fire environment on the breakage of glass
8	Blight, G. E. 1974	Exp.[L]	— heated glass by insertion into a hot cabinet — compares heat absorption of clear and reflective glass; clear glass absorbs less, ∴ remains cooler, ∴ less susceptible to thermal fracture — use demac gauge (demountable) for strain measurements **Output:** a. glass is isotropic but β increases with increasing temperature for T > 60°C b. stress in shaded edge is uniaxial tension parallel to edge. In the heated area stress is uniaxial compression parallel to edge. In the corners stress approximates to an isotropic compression. c. by using Griffith criterion $\varepsilon t = \textbf{const.}$ $(\gamma/EC)^{1/2}$ explains why cracks initiate at edge and are controlled by defects. d. stress in shaded edge increases with increasing edge width. e. there is a size effect with induced edge strains increasing with increasing glass size. f. recommends the use of a conducting strip to direct heat into the shaded region to minimize thermal stress.
9	Stahn, D. 1980	Analyt.[L]	— by finite element technique using solid SAP (Static Analysis Prog.) predicts thermal stresses for various temperature distributions imposed by different shadow geometries **Output:** a. thermal stress is constant over majority of edge length and reduces to zero at corners b. tensile stresses at the edges are equal to principle stresses except at corners ∴ these can be directly used for safety assessments

#	Author	Type	Description
10	Mai, Y. W. Jacob, L. J. S. 1979	Analyt.[L] and Exp.[L]	— use of stress analysis (partial differential equations determined numerically to predict stress from σ = **const. E$\beta\Delta$T** — use of fracture mechanics, concepts to predict stress from $\sigma_f = 2.24 \dfrac{K_{ic}}{\sqrt{r}}$ where; K_{ic} = stress intensity factor, r = mirror radius of fracture — experimental evaluation of stress in the glass utilizing strain gauges output: a. experimental and predicted values of stress agreed well b. shadows increase thermal stresses by 10% c. the use of thermal conductive sealant is suggested
11	Pilette, C. F. Taylor, D. A.	Analyt.[L]	— uses finite element analysis to investigate the effect of varying parameters on thermal stresses in double glazed windows — model: three dimensional solid elements for sealant and gasket and thin shell element for glass. parameters investigated: window size, frame absorption, outdoor air temperature, gasket, solar heat flux, sealant stiffness, exterior air film conductance, influence of vertical and horizontal shadows **Output:** a. maximum thermal stress occurs along the edge where shadow line intersects the edge. b. three dimensional effect in a double glazed window are negligible, i.e, in plane forces are not transmitted to other pane
12	Joshi, A. A. Pagni, P. J. 1994	Analyt.[L]	Glass thermal field obtained from model in ref. 5 are examined. **Output:** a. glass surface temperature increasing with decreasing decay length of flame radiation b. glass surface temperature increasing with decreasing flame radiation heat flux c. breaking time decreasing with increasing shaded width d. breaking time decreasing with increasing decay length f. most of imposed heat influx is stored in the glass, increasing its temperature

Appendix I. (Cont'd.)

No.	Author and Date	Type of Paper[a]	Executive Summary
13	N. A. McArthur 1991	Exp.[L]	— an investigation into the performance of windows with aluminium and wooden frames subjected to bush fire — furnace and standard time-temperature curve was used as the means of heating **Output:** a. time to fracture b. crack and bifurcation patterns c. fracture face observation d. Comparison of performance of aluminium and wooden window frames subjected to bush fire conditions.
14	Joshi, A. A. Pagni, P. J. 1994	Exp.[L]	— use of four point bend test method and Weibull analysis to determine the breaking stress of glass **Output:** a. $\sigma_f \approx 40$ MPa b. Weibull parameters; $m = 1.21$, $\sigma_0 = 33$ MPa, $\sigma_u = 35.8$ MPa c. the results of Skelly's experiments (Ref. 6) are compared with Pagni's BREAK programme (Ref. 4) and found good agreement
15	Cuzzilo, B. Pagni, P. J. 1992	Analyt.[L]	— describe Joshi and Pagni's work (Ref. 2) — applies the method to a double paned window subjected to a wild fire **Output:** a. the pane farther from fire stays cool, if the pane facing fire were to break and fall out then the cool pane begins to heat up and break b. fire facing pane with low-E coating will stay cool enough to avoid breaking
16	Emmons, H. W. 1988	Analyt.[L] Review	— review of O. Keski-Rahkonen's work (Ref. 3) to predict glass crack initiation — draws attention to distinction of "crack growth" from "Crack Initiations" — suggests that $\sigma_Y = E. \beta (T_\infty\ T_0)$ be experimentally validated, especially stress measurement at the glass edge is requested — puts forward an explanation for crack bifurcation based on beam theory

| 17 | Hassani, S. K. S. Sheilds, T. J. Silcock, G. W. (Due to be Published) | Exp.[L] | — Experimental evaluation of thermal and stress field in glazing units subjected to real fires.
— Thermal strains were measured in-situ using strain gauges.

Output:
a. experimental determination of dynamic stress development in glazing subjected to real fires. |
| 18 | Sheilds, T. J. Silcock, G. W. Braniff, J. 1992 | Exp.[L] | — experimental investigation of performance of double glazed window units in enclosure fires. The glazing units were specially constructed to incorporate thermocouples to monitor surface temperatures on all of the glazing surfaces.

Output:
a. Data in graphical form depicting the temporal variation of surface temperatures, associated gas temperature variations with respect to time in both the descending hot gas layer and lower cool zone. |

[a]Exp.[L] = Experimental, Analyt.[L] = Analytical.

REFERENCES

1. H. W. Emmons, The Needed Fire Science, in *Fire Safety Science—Proceedings of the First International Symposium*, C. E. Grant and P. J. Pagni (eds.), Hemisphere, Washington, D.C., pp. 33-53, 1986.
2. A. Joshi and P. J. Pagni, Thermal Analysis of a Compartment Fire on Window Glass, *Report No. NIST-GCR-90-576*, June 1990.
3. O. Keski-Rahkonen, Breaking of Glass Close to Fire, I, *Fire and Materials, 12*, pp. 61-69, 1988.
4. A. A. Joshi and P. J. Pagni, Users' Guide to Break1, The Berkeley Algorithm for Breaking Window Glass in a Compartment Fire, *Report No. NIST-GCR-91-596*, October 1991.
5. P. J. Pagni and A. A. Joshi, Glass Breaking in Fires, *Proceedings of Third International Symposium on Fire Safety Science*, pp. 791-802, 1991.
6. M. J. Shelly, R. J. Roby, and C. L. Beyler, An Experimental Investigation of Glass Breakage in Compartment Fires, *Journal of Fire Protection Engineering, 3*:1, pp. 25-34, 1991.
7. G. W. H. Silcock and T. J. Shields, An Experimental Evaluation of Glazing in Compartment Fires, *Interflam 93, Proceedings of the Sixth International Interflam Conference*, pp. 747-756, 1993.
8. G. E. Blight, Thermal Strain and Fracture of Building Glass, *First Australian Conference on Engineering Materials*, NSW University, NSW, pp. 685-700, 1974.
9. D. Stahn, Thermal Stresses in Heat-absorbing Building Glass Subjected to Solar Radiation, *Proceedings, International Conference on Thermal Stresses in Materials and Structures in Severe Thermal Environment*, Virginia Polytechnic and State University, Blacksburg, Virginia, pp. 305-323, March 1980.
10. Y. W. Mai and L. J. S. Jacob, Thermal Stress Fracture of Solar Control Window Panes Caused by Shading of Incident Radiation, *Materiaux et Constructions, 13*:76, pp. 283-288, 1980.
11. C. F. Pilette and D. A. Taylor, Thermal Stresses in Double-glazed Windows, *Construction Engineering, 15*:5, pp. 807-814, 1988.
12. A. A. Joshi and P. J. Pagni, Fire-Induced Thermal Fields in Window Glass, I-Theory, *Fire Safety Journal, 22*, pp. 25-43, 1994.
13. N. A. McArthur, The Performance of Aluminium Building Products in Bushfires, *Fire and Materials, 15*, pp. 117-125, 1991.
14. A. A. Joshi and P. J. Pagni, Fire-induced Thermal Fields in Window Glass, II-Experiments, *Fire Safety Journal, 22*, pp. 45-65, 1994.
15. B. Cuzzillo and P. J. Pagni, Windows in Wildfires, *Wind and Fire II,* Abstracts of Students Research Projects, Course ME 290F, Case Histories, University of California, Berkeley, Spring 1992.
16. H. W. Emmons, Window Glass Breakage by Fire, *Home Fire Project Technical Report No. 77*, Harvard University, Cambridge, Massachusetts, 1988.
17. S. K. S. Hassani, T. J. Shields, and G. W. Silcock, Experimental Evaluation of Temperature and Stress Field in Glass Subjected to an Enclosure Fire (in press).

18. T. J. Shields, G. W. H. Silcock, and J. M. Braniff, Building Regulation *Interaction Report, 1*, Fire Research Centre, University of Ulster, September 1992.
19. T. J. Shields and G. W. Silcock, *Performance of Glazing in Enclosure Fires,* Private Research Report, Fire SERT Centre, University of Ulster, 1992.

CHAPTER 3

In Situ Experimental Thermal Stress Measurements in Glass Subjected to Enclosure Fires

S. K. S. Hassani, T. J. Shields, and G. W. H. Silcock

A number of experimental studies carried out by the authors have indicated that the glass in an enclosure fire may be subjected to a non-uniform thermal environment and the glazing unit may stay in place much longer after the onset of the first crack. The results of these real fire tests highlighted the need for experimental investigation of the state of thermal stress in glazing systems subjected to various thermal environments. In these studies, in-situ thermal strain in the glass subjected to both uniform and non-uniform gas temperatures were measured utilizing strain gauges. This chapter discusses the experimental technique for utilization of strain gauges which may be used as a tool to assess the behavior of glazing systems in enclosure fires. Gauge installation and signal processing to obtain reliable data are demonstrated. The interpretation of results obtained by this method by relating to the physical conditions within the fire enclosure and in the glass pane at the time of glass cracking is also demonstrated. This technique can be used to obtain useful experimental data for input to fire simulation modeling and risk analysis.

In ventilation controlled room fires, the growth and development of the fire may be partly dependant on whether the window glazing in the room will stay in place or disintegrate. Traditionally, designers have assumed that the area of window glazing can be equated to a vent (i.e., assume that glazing has collapsed completely) when the upper layer gas temperature has exceeded 600°C. In recent modeling work [1, 2], attempts have been made to predict the performance of the glazing based on the temperature distribution in the glass. However, these mathematical models require validation using reliable experimental data.

The principal aim of this chapter is to discuss an experimental methodology for evaluation of the thermal stress developed in window glass subjected to the thermal insult from a growing enclosure fire. The use of experimental results to indicate important events affecting the performance of the glazing is demonstrated. The capabilities of existing models to reflect these real events is also discussed.

THE DEVELOPMENT OF EDGE STRESSES

It is well known that a sheet of glass shielded around the edges from the thermal insult of a heating environment consisting of convecting hot gases, radiation from flames and hot surfaces, will be placed in tension along its edges. This is caused by a differential expansion rate due to the fact that the temperature in the exposed section of the glass is greater than that in the shaded section. The mismatch in thermal expansion of the exposed section of the glass and the shaded edge section causes cracks to initiate at the edges where it is known that the highest tensile stresses occur.

Recent experimental work has confirmed in a more general sense that the position of initial cracks and subsequent crack bifurcation routes depend on local temperature differences in the glass [3]. Also, temperature variations in a glass pane can be complex, since they depend on compartment gas temperature distribution (hot and cold zones), location of the glazing with respect to the fire and the degree of glass exposure to the fire environment (edge shielding by the frame). This indicates that the current analytical solutions used to predict the thermal field in the glass based on simple idealized boundary conditions need further development. Thus to further the understanding of the complex processes involved it is necessary to provide a set of sound experimentally derived data in order to both validate current analysis methods and to assist in the formulation of future models.

EXPERIMENTAL METHODOLOGY

In the following sections the details of an experimental methodology will be outlined whereby it is possible to obtain surface temperatures and thermally induced edge stresses. Special considerations regarding the use of strain gauges at elevated temperatures will also be discussed. Examples of experimental results will be demonstrated which may be used to validate theories and analytical methods.

Temperature Field Evaluation

An array of type K mineral insulated thermocouples with inconel sheaths and junction near the physical tip were used to determine the glass surface temperatures. Utilizing the flexibility of the sheath material the thermocouples could be formed into coil like arrangements, see Figure 1, which make it possible to position and secure the thermocouples tips on the glass, enabling the surface

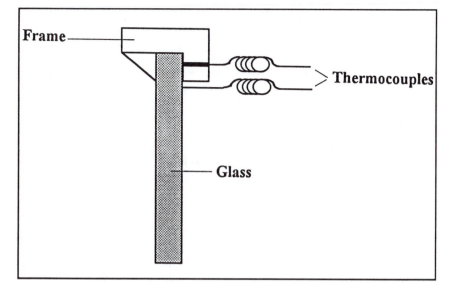

Figure 1. Details of thermocouples mounting in the shaded
and exposed regions of the glass.

temperatures in the shaded and exposed region of the glass to be measured. The results from this strategically located array of thermocouples yielded local temperature differences and also enabled a profile of the thermal field in the glass to be determined. The data from the thermocouples were collected and recorded using a personal computer based data acquisition system. For example Figure 2 shows the local temperature in the shaded region of the upper glass edge and the adjacent exposed surface temperature close to the frame. Also shown is the local temperature difference between these two points as the fire develops. The quantitative evaluation of temperature difference between the edge regions and the exposed sections is considered to be an important parameter required for the development of analytical models.

By increasing the number of thermocouples it should be possible to plot a more well-defined dynamic map of the surface temperatures. Thus, the effect of varying parameters such as fire position, ventilation, position of the window, etc., can be systematically investigated.

Stress Field Evaluation

From a literature survey on the measurement and analysis of thermal stress in solar control glazing systems [4] useful information was distilled on the type of stress distributions expected in glazing subjected to a steady and varying thermal

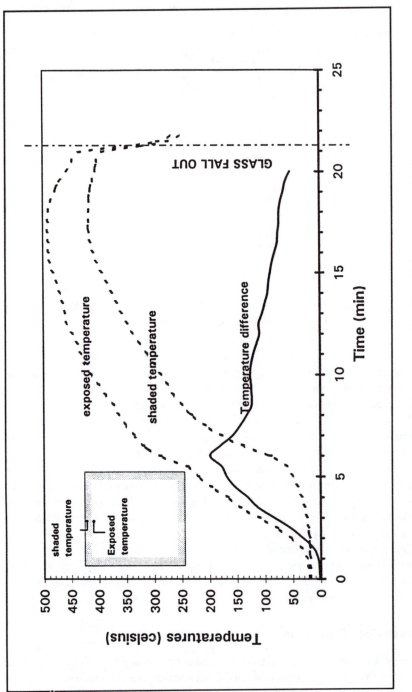

Figure 2. Local shaded and exposed and the differential temperatures Vs time.

flux. Since the maximum tensile stresses occur near to and in a direction parallel to the edges, it was determined that the strain gauges needed to be placed along and as close to the glass edge as possible in order to record the maximum failure inducing tensile stress, see Figure 3. It also proved convenient that this location was shielded due to protection offered by the framing from the high temperatures expected in the exposed regions and from direct contact with the hostile enclosure fire environment. Thus it was possible to keep the gauge at an acceptable temperature during the development of critical thermally induced edge strains.

In locating strain gauges in the edge region of double glazing units it was necessary to evaluate the possibility of installing the gauges in the ambient side of the glazing system. Therefore a series of tests were carried out using a single sheet of glass to establish whether the thermally induced strains measured at both sides of glass edge, one on the fire side and the other on the ambient side, would yield similar results. Figure 4 shows the edge strain variation with time measured at two points on the surface opposite to each other in the shaded edge section. It is

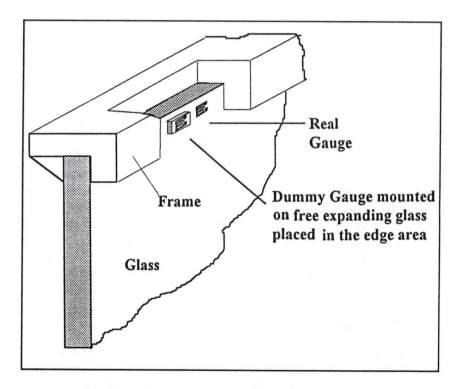

Figure 3. Details of strain gauges mounted in the shaded region of window glass.

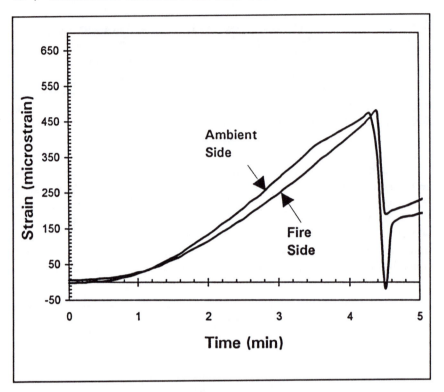

Figure 4. Comparison of measured strain from inner (fire) surface
and the outer (ambient) surface of glass pane.

clear from the results that the strain levels are very similar indicating that strain measurements can be taken from either side of the glass edge. This makes it possible to install the gauges on the ambient side which is much preferred since they are readily accessible and the connecting wires do not have to be protected against the hostile fire environment. It is also most convenient when installing gauges on double glazing units since it is possible to attach the gauges to the external faces of the system, see Figure 5.

Strain Gauge Considerations

The installation of strain gauges for use at elevated temperatures is not a straightforward task and it becomes even more complicated when the strain gauge has to be mounted on a glass surface which is inherently smooth and chemically inactive. Thus details of an experimentally proven method of strain gauge installation on a glass surface will be given in the following section.

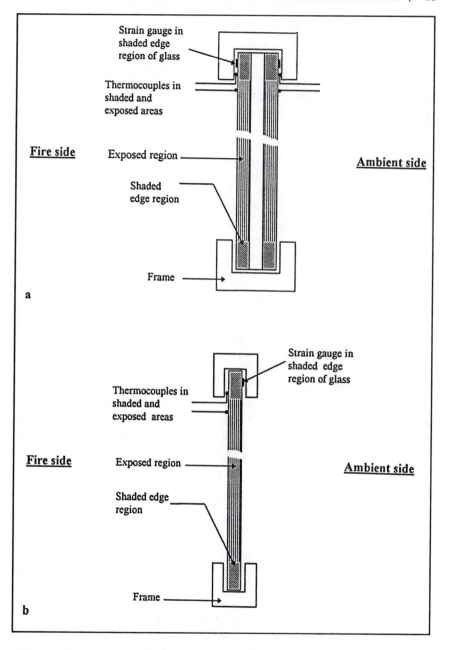

Figure 5. (a) Schematic representation of double glazing unit showing instruments arrangements. (b) Schematic representation of single glazing showing instruments arrangements.

Strain Gauge Installation

Initially the area on the surface where a strain gauge had to be mounted needed to be physically and chemically clean if a sound bond was to be achieved. Such a clean surface condition may be obtained by grinding the surface with a 400 grit emery paper and conditioning and neutralizing it with suitable chemicals. Once a clean surface was available the strain gauge was aligned with the longitudinal axis parallel to the edge and located as close as possible to the edge. Cellophane tape was used to locate and fix the gauge in place prior to application of a carefully selected adhesive between the gauge and the glass surface. The gauge was then pressed down and held using clamps for a pre-determined time to allow the adhesive to cure. It was of paramount importance to choose a suitable adhesive that would operate in the environment that the gauge is subjected to, which in this case was the working temperature limit. Once the adhesive had cured connection wires were soldered on to the integral tabs provided. Thus using the above method of gauge installation single and multiple glazing systems were successfully instrumented.

Glass Mounting and Framing Considerations

The instrumented glass was secured in the frame by a light clamping action which provided an evenly distributed load along the edges. The glass was insulated and sealed in the frame using a ceramic wool insulating blanket material and strips of insulating calcium silicate board. The strips of insulating board also facilitate the positioning of the pane of glass in the frame such that there was a uniform width of glass edge shaded by the frame. The pane of glass was uniformly supported along its lower edge and was allowed to expand in its plane thereby eliminating the influence of the frame as an external constraint during the test period.

Gauge Thermal Output Compensation

The signal indicated by the gauge installed in the shaded part of the glass pane is the compound strain comprised of three distinct components:

1. Gauge thermal output which is due to the change in the resistivity of the gauge with respect to a change of the temperature. The resulting change in the gauge resistance is indicated as a strain which has to be separated from the net physical strain.
2. The free expansion of the glass with respect to temperature change. This free expansion is due to the heating of the glass which is indicated by the gauge in the form of strain not related to any physical stress.
3. The physical strain due to thermally induced stresses caused by thermal mismatch within the body of the glass pane. This internal physical stress places the edge region in the state of tension and may ultimately result in the failure of the glass.

Clearly the strains indicated in items (1) and (2) above are artefacts of instrumentation and a non-stress related strain, and must be separated from the thermally induced strain in item (3) which is needed for stress analysis.

To this end a dummy gauge was mounted on a small piece of glass similar to the instrumented pane and incorporated in the shaded region under the frame, Figure 3, so that it experienced the same thermal environment as the active gauge. Noting that the small piece of glass was subjected to the same local uniform temperature as the active gauge it would experience a free expansion equal to that in the glass pane without experiencing the internal thermal stresses, i.e., the dummy gauge only indicated the strains described in items (1) and (2) above. Therefore by subtracting the dummy gauge response from the active gauge response by way of a wheatstone bridge network where each gauge forms an adjacent arm in a half bridge circuit configuration the net physical strain was obtained.

STRAIN GAUGE OUTPUT DATA

Using the technique outlined previously a profile of the dynamic development of thermal strains in the single glazed sheet of dimensions 965 mm × 787 mm incorporated in a fire enclosure 1600 mm (H) × 1700 mm (W) × 1500 mm (D) was obtained by charting the response of compensated strain gauge output with respect to time as shown in Figure 6. In this case the fire in the enclosure was located in the corner. As shown in Figure 6 the strain level in the top edge of the glazing increased with time to a critical level at which the cracking occurred indicated by a sharp fall in the strain level. The associated stresses induced in the glazing could then be determined by utilizing the experimentally derived strain value and the simple elastic theory.

i.e., σ (stress) = E (young's modulus). ε (strain). (1)

EXPERIMENTAL VALIDATION OF CURRENT THEORIES

When attempting to model glass failure the main relationship researchers [1, 2] used was:

$$\sigma = E.\beta.\Delta T \tag{2}$$

with strain ε expressed as

$$\varepsilon = \beta.\Delta T \tag{3}$$

In equation (3) β is coefficient of thermal expansion, and ΔT is temperature difference existing between temperature at the center of glazing and that in the shaded edge region.

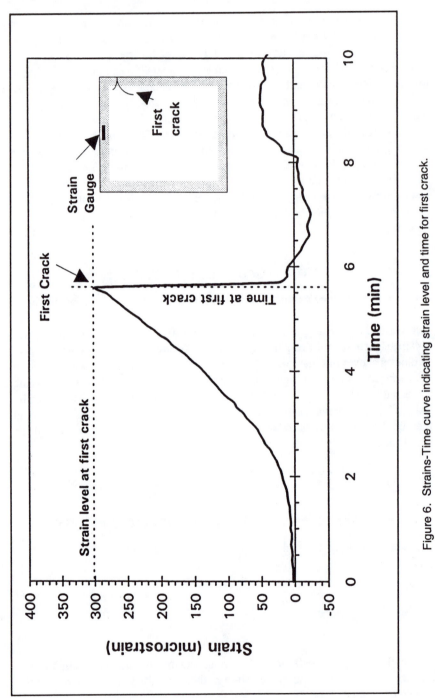

Figure 6. Strains-Time curve indicating strain level and time for first crack.

Two of the key assumptions central to the analysis reported in [1, 2] were that the temperature profile in the plane of glass is uniform in the exposed section and that in the shaded edge regions the temperatures remained uniform and very close to the initial temperature. The transition from the temperatures prevailing in the exposed region to that in the shaded regions when the window is about to break are approximated [1] by either a hyperbolic tangent or a step function. Using these key assumptions it was concluded that only the glass central temperature was needed to estimate the glass breaking stress. During the course of a large number of tests [3, 5] utilizing large glazing systems exposed to enclosure fires it was concluded that the temperature profiles in the glazing both in the shaded and in exposed sections were not uniform. Also it was found that the edge temperatures rose considerably from the initial temperature implying that the local shaded/ unshaded temperature differences more appropriately reflect the term ΔT. Such observations and findings place the previously held key assumption that the same constant ΔT value holds for the entire glass edge in doubt. For example, for large windows situated at some distance from the fire bed and subjected to a two zone thermal environment, the local shaded/unshaded temperature difference in the top section of the window is expected to be much greater than that in the lower section. However, in a situation where the window is adjacent to the fire bed, absorption of radiation from the flames may be the major mechanism for the glass heating compared to hot gas convection transfer. This suggests that the section of glass closer to the fire bed will be heated at a higher rate than the more remote sections for some period of time during the fire development. Therefore, in analyzing thermally induced stresses in glazing subjected to an enclosure fire local temperature differences will need to be considered. Only then will it be possible to obtain a more realistic prediction of edge stress in the pane of glass.

CONCLUSIONS

- Actual in-situ edge stresses in a pane of glass subjected to a non uniform thermal environment can be readily obtained using thermally compensated strain gauges that can be fixed to the glass surface in the shaded edge region.
- Strain gauges can be mounted in the edge region on either side of glass pane since it has been established that the strain level measured on both sides are similar.
- Heat transfer in the glazing system subjected to enclosure fires is complex. A sound experimental method now exists for collection of relevant data necessary for a more complete understanding of the edge cracking process and the subsequent development of analytical models.

REFERENCES

1. P. J. Pagni and A. A. Joshi, Glass Breaking in Fires, *Proceedings of Third International Symposium on Fire Safety Science*, pp. 791-802, 1991.
2. O. Keski-Rahkonen, Breaking of Glass Close to Fire, I, *Fire and Materials, 12*, pp. 61-69, 1988.
3. S. K. S. Hassani, T. J. Shields, and G. W. Silcock, An Experimental Investigation into the Behaviour of Glazing, *Journal of Applied Fire Science, 4*:4, pp. 303-323, 1995.
4. S. K. S. Hassani, T. J. Shields, and G. W. Silcock, Thermal Fracture of Window Glazing: Performance of Glazing, *Journal of Applied Fire Science, 4*:4, pp. 249-263, 1995.
5. G. W. H. Silcock and T. J. Shields, An Experimental Evaluation of Glazing in Compartment Fires, *Interflam 93, Proceedings of the Sixth International Interflam Conference*, pp. 747-756, 1993.

CHAPTER 4

The Behavior of Single Glazing in an Enclosure Fire

T. J. Shields, G. W. H. Silcock, and S. K. S. Hassani

In order to advance work in progress at the University of Ulster [1] on the behavior of glazing systems during real fires in enclosures, an experimental research program was undertaken to study the behaviors of single and double pane window glazing systems. This chapter discusses the results obtained in experiments using single glazing with respect to location of fire source, position of glazing, and the effect of the descending hot gas layer. The temperature and induced stress fields in the glass time to first fracture, crack bifurcation patterns, and extent of glass fallout are reported and discussed.

EXPERIMENTAL FACILITY

A fire compartment 1.7 m high, 1.5 m wide, and 1.6 m deep was constructed and instrumented as shown in Figure 1. The enclosure walls were 100 mm concrete block work, the roof consisted of 115 mm reinforced concrete with 15 mm thick insulation board fixed to the underside, and the concrete floor was covered with 15 mm thick insulation board. An adjustable vent was provided in one corner of the room with an adjacent tree of thermocouples to measure the inlet and outlet gas temperatures. The vent was 1240 mm high × 120 mm wide. The fuel source for these experiments was wood cribs mounted on a load cell with the latter arranged so that it could be positioned in a corner or center of the room. The wood crib measured approximately 500 mm × 500 mm × 500 mm and was arranged in an eight 30 mm × 30 mm stick high stack with 30 mm spacing. The total mass of the fuel was approximately 19.0 kg. In order to investigate the effect of the location of the fire, the wood cribs were located in the center and in a corner of the room.

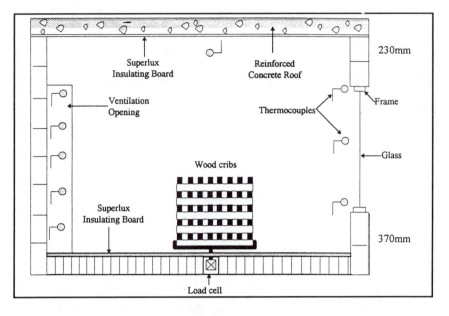

Figure 1. Instrumented experimental room: single glazing experiments.

A window arrangement was built into the enclosure with temperature compensated strain gauges [2] and thermocouples positioned as shown in Figure 2. The window arrangement was such that during the tests one of the panes was totally immersed in the hot gas layer shortly after the fuel was ignited whereas the tall pane was subjected to a two zone environment. The glass used in the experiments was 6 mm thick ordinary float glass.

The gas temperature profiles within the room and the shaded and exposed glass surface temperatures were measured using type K sheathed thermocouples, Figures 1 through 3. Temperature compensated strain gauges were used to measure the thermally induced edge-strains in the glass, Figure 3 [2].

Three experiments were conducted with single glazing varying the parameters as shown in Table 1.

RESULTS AND OBSERVATIONS

Summary of Results

The results obtained from the three experiments with respect to the occurrence of the first and second cracks, crack location, and extent of glass fallout are summarized in Table 2.

The location of cracking and crack bifurcations are shown in Figures 4 through 6.

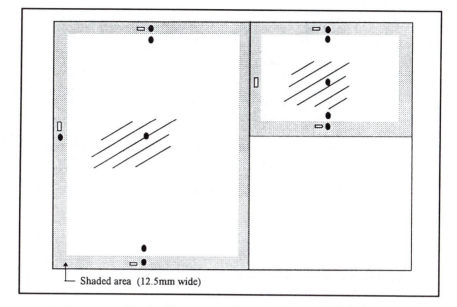

Figure 2. Window arrangement, dimensions, and instrumentation: single glazing.

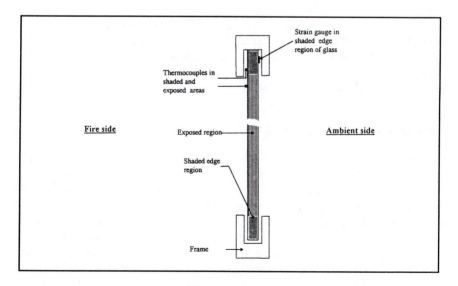

Figure 3. Schematic representation of single glazing showing arrangement of instruments.

Table 1. Single Glazing Experiments (6 mm glass) by Position of Fire
in Enclosure and Ventilation Rates

Experiment	Type of Glazing	Fire Load Type/Weight	Position of Fire Load	Ventilation Opening
1	Single	Wood crib 19.1 kg	Center	Full open vent
2	Single	Wood crib 19.1 kg	Center	Reduced ventilation area of vent: 1030 mm × 83 mm
3	Single	Wood crib 19.1 kg	Corner	Full open vent

Enclosure Gas Temperature Profiles

The enclosure gas temperature profiles for the experiments listed in Table 1 are presented in Figures 7 through 9.

The temperature differences over the depth of the hot gas layers depicted by thermocouples numbers 1 and 3 for experiments 1 and 3 will be noted bearing in mind that for experiment 3 the fire was in the corner location. It would appear that the effect of the induced upper gas layer flow patterns and possible mixing associated with the corner fire is to significantly reduce the temperature difference over the hot gas layer depth. Further, the hot gas layer temperatures continue to gradually increase in experiment number 3, whereas in experiment number 1 they tend toward steady state conditions suggesting that the location of the fire may affect the manner in which the glazing heats up.

Exposed Glass Surface Temperatures

The glass surface temperatures recorded for the large and small panes are presented in Figures 10 through 15.

For experiments 1 and 2, the fire is in the center of the room approximately 1 m from the glazing. In experiment 1 the temperatures recorded at the center of the large pane are higher than those recorded at the top of the large pane practically over the whole duration of the experiment. It would appear that radiation from the flame and fuel bed is the dominant mode of heat transfer. In experiment 3 the glass temperatures recorded are much higher than those recorded in the other two experiments. Similar patterns are apparent for the small glass panes although the temperature changes across the exposed surface of the small glass pane are smaller.

Table 2. Summary of Results for Single Glazing by Time to First and Second Cracking, Crack Location, Loss of Integrity Measured Edge Strains, and Loss of Integrity

Experiment	Time to first crack (mins)		Time to second crack (mins)		Measured Edge Strains at Cracking (με) Large Pane		Measured Edge Strains at Cracking (με) Small Pane		Time to Loss of Integrity (mins)		Percent Glass Fallout	
	Large Pane	Small Pane	Large Pane	Small Pane	First Crack	Second Crack	First Crack	Second Crack	Large Pane	Small Pane	Large Pane	Small Pane
1	4.1	4.5	5.0	5.7	290	280	480	680	0	0	0	0
2	5.1	5.2	12.35	6.6	230	80	550	370	0	0	0	0
3	5.6	5.5	11.70	6.8	300	70	290	100	19.9	11.4	100	3

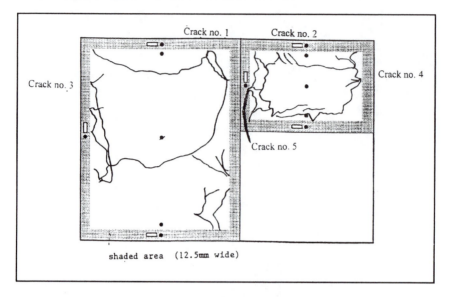

Figure 4. Experiment 1: Single glazing, time, sequence, and location of cracking and crack bifurcation patterns.

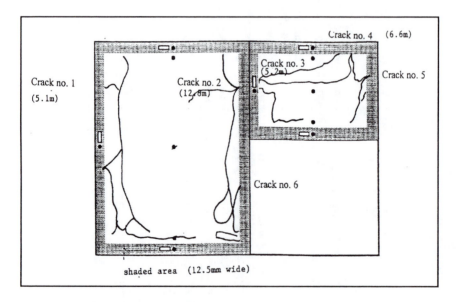

Figure 5. Experiment 2: Single glazing, time, sequence, and location of cracking and crack bifurcation patterns.

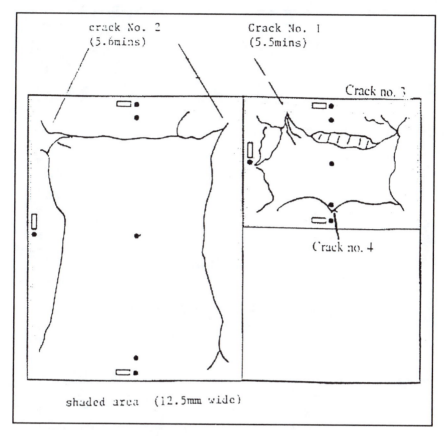

crack No. 2
(5.6mins)

Crack No. 1
(5.5mins)

Crack no. 3

Crack no. 4

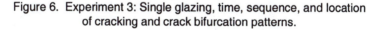

shaded area   (12.5mm wide)

Figure 6. Experiment 3: Single glazing, time, sequence, and location
of cracking and crack bifurcation patterns.

Shaded Glass Temperatures

The shaded glass temperatures recorded at locations given in Figure 3 for the large and small glass panes are presented in Figures 16 through 21.

With the exception of experiment 2, the shaded edge temperatures all follow the same order top, middle, and bottom, regarding the magnitude of the recorded temperatures.

Thermally Induced Strains

The recorded thermally induced strains for the large and small panes are presented in Figures 22 through 27.

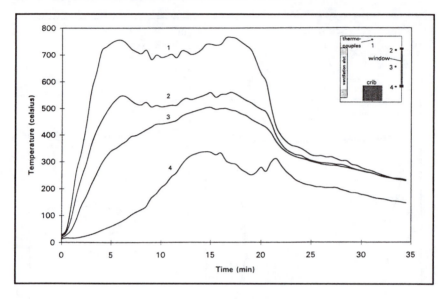

Figure 7. Experiment No. 1: Gas temperature profile in the fire enclosure.

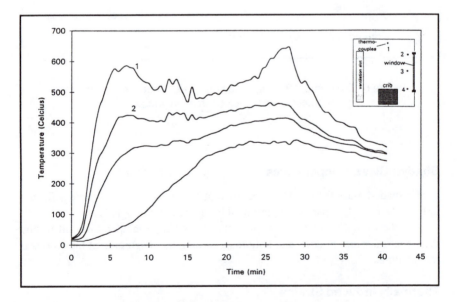

Figure 8. Experiment No. 2: Gas temperature profile in the fire enclosure.

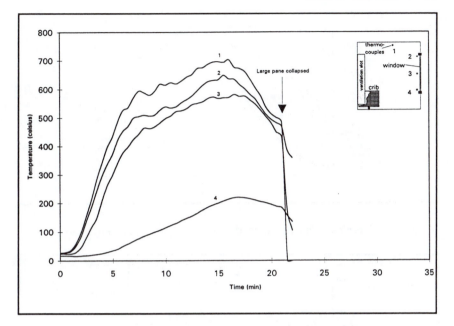

Figure 9. Experiment No. 3: Gas temperature profile in the
fire enclosure.

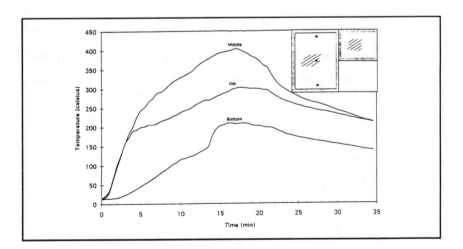

Figure 10. Experiment No. 1:
Exposed surface temperatures: large glass pane.

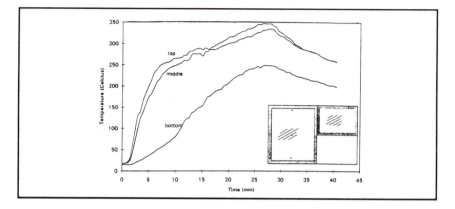

Figure 11. Experiment No. 2: Exposed surface temperatures: large glass pane.

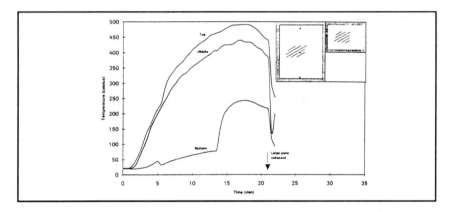

Figure 12. Experiment No. 3: Exposed surface temperatures: large glass pane.

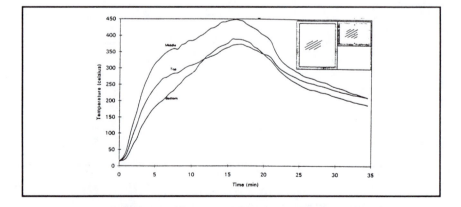

Figure 13. Experiment No. 1: Exposed surface temperatures: small glass pane.

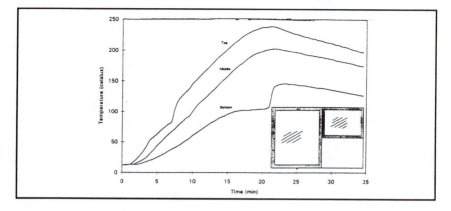

Figure 14. Experiment No. 2: Exposed surface temperatures: small glass pane.

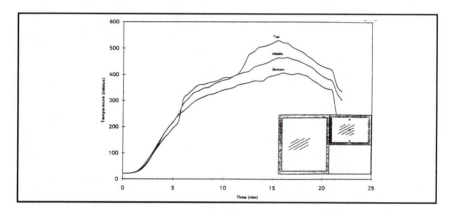

Figure 15. Experiment No. 3: Exposed surface temperatures: small glass pane.

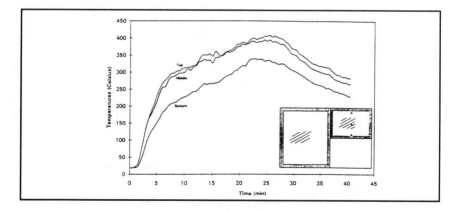

Figure 16. Experiment No. 1: Shaded edge temperatures: large glass pane.

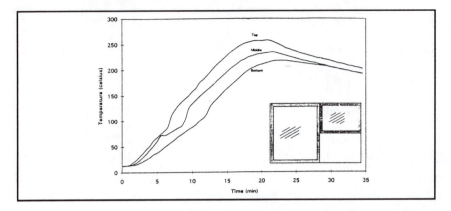

Figure 17. Experiment No. 2: Shaded edge temperatures: large glass pane.

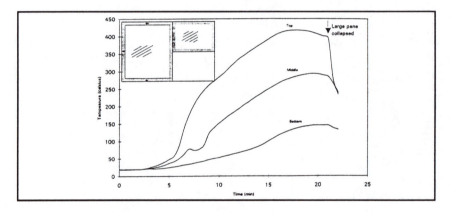

Figure 18. Experiment No. 3: Shaded edge temperatures: large glass pane.

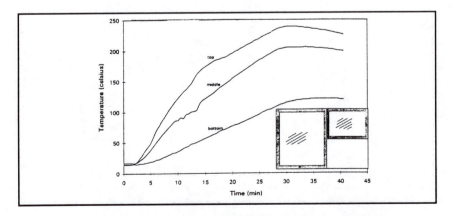

Figure 19. Experiment No. 1: Shaded edge temperatures: small glass pane.

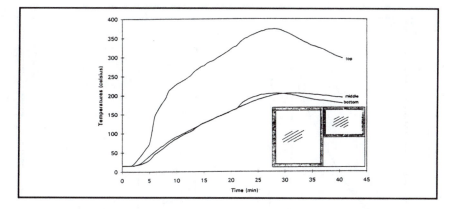

Figure 20. Experiment No. 2: Shaded edge temperatures: small glass pane.

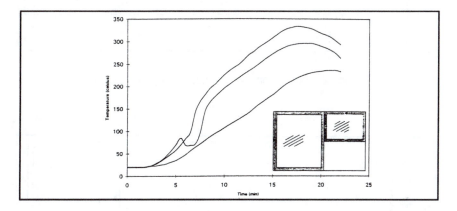

Figure 21. Experiment No. 3: Shaded edge temperatures: small glass pane.

The differences in the magnitude of measured edge strains for the small and large panes will be noted.

ANALYSIS OF RESULTS

In experiment 1, the fire source was located in the center of the room and full ventilation was employed. It was established from the gas temperature profile at the ventilation opening that the hot gas layer descended to approximately the height of the top of the fuel bed, i.e., 450 mm above the floor.

The times for the first and subsequent cracks for the large and small panes to occur are given in Table 2. The upper gas layer temperature when the first crack occurred was 715°C. For both the large and small panes the first crack occurred in the vicinity of strain gauge number 1 located at the top edge of the pane. The

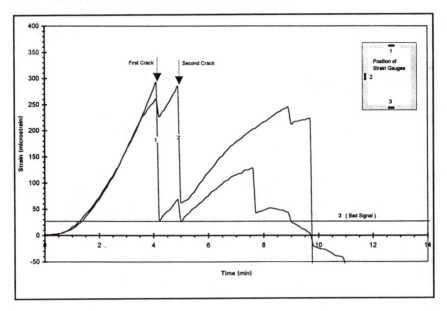

Figure 22. Experiment No. 1: Strains: large glass pane.

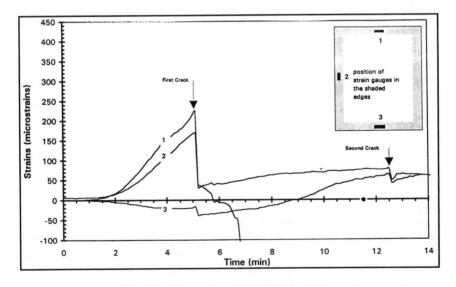

Figure 23. Experiment No. 2: Strains: large glass pane.

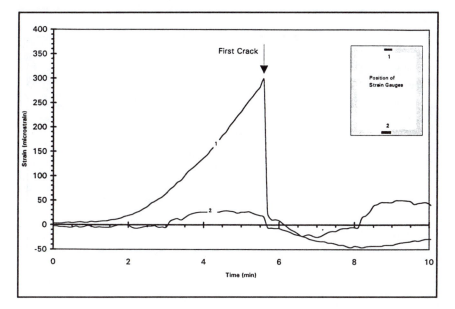

Figure 24. Experiment No. 3: Strains: large glass pane.

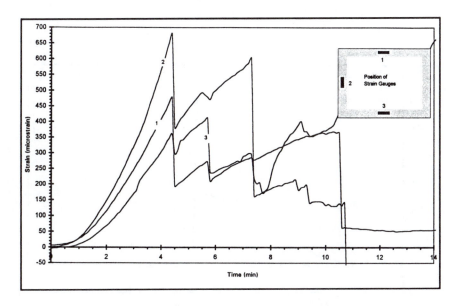

Figure 25. Experiment No. 1: Strains: small glass pane.

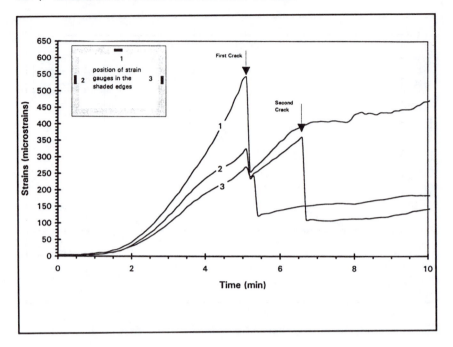

Figure 26. Experiment No. 2: Strains: small glass pane.

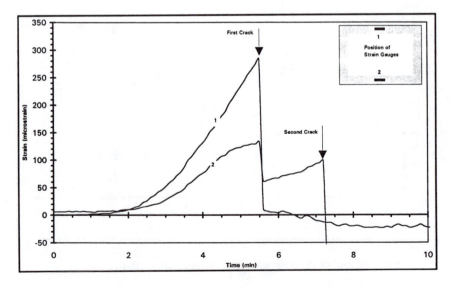

Figure 27. Experiment No. 3: Strains: small glass pane.

recorded strains for the small and large panes at the time of the first cracks were 480 and 300 micro strains respectively. The temperature difference between the glass surface temperature and the shaded edge temperature for the top edges of the large and small panes was approximately 150°C.

An examination of Figures 10 and 13 that relate to experiment 1 indicates that the middle sections of the glass panes were hotter during the experiments than the top section of the panes. Given the location of the fuel bed in the center of the room, the distance of the fuel bed from the glazing (1 m), and the nature of the fuel, it follows that radiation from the fuel bed and flames was the dominant mode of heat transfer. Consequently, the middle sections of the glazing systems, due to in-depth absorption of radiation, realized higher temperatures.

In the second experiment, the fire source is located in the center of the room, and subjected to reduced ventilation. It was established from the gas temperature profile at the ventilation opening that the hot gas layer descended again to approximately the top of the fuel bed, behavior similar to that observed in experiment 1.

The extent of cracking in both the large and small panes during experiment 2 is illustrated in Figure 5. Also, the times to the occurrence of the first and subsequent cracks for the large and small panes are given in Table 2.

From Figures 23 and 24 respectively, the first crack occurred in the vicinity of strain gauge number 1 located at the top edges of the panes, for both the large and small panes, where the upper gas layer temperature was approximately 600°C, much lower than in experiment 1. The recorded strains for the large and small panes at the time of cracking were 230 micro strain and 550 micro strain, respectively. The temperature difference between the exposed glass surface temperature and the shaded edge temperature for the top edges of the large and small panes at the time of the first crack occurring was 150°C. Examination of Figures 11 and 14 shows the top and middle exposed glass surface temperatures to be similar, suggesting immersion in the hot gas layer where convective heating is dominating the process. The extent of cracking in both the large and small panes is illustrated in Figure 5.

In experiment 3, the fuel source was placed in the corner with room full ventilation operating where it was established from the gas temperature profiles at the ventilation opening that the hot gas layer had again descended to approximately the top of the fuel bed.

From Figure 9 it can be concluded that the upper gas layer temperature when the first crack occurred was 530°C. Also, for both the large and small panes, the first crack occurred in the vicinity of strain gauge number 1 located at the top edge of the pane. The recorded strains for the large and small panes at the time of the first cracks, Figures 24 and 27, were 300 micro strains and 290 micro strains, respectively.

The difference between the exposed glass surface temperature and the shaded edge temperature for the top edges of the large and small panes was 190°C.

An inspection of Figures 22 through 27 will indicate that generally the variations in edge strain with respect to time for the three experiments have broadly similar profiles. For the large glass panes, the measured edge strains range from 200 micro strain to 300 micro strain. For the small panes the measured edge strains range from 300 micro strain to 700 micro strain, implying that tensile stress values exhibited the following ranges, i.e., 16 MPa-24 MPa and 24 MPa and 56 MPa for the large and small panes, respectively. These variations in tensile stress on face value suggest that the small panes are harder to crack than the larger ones under the same level of thermal insult

In this regard, Figures 4 through 6 and Table 2 give details regarding the extent of loss of integrity for the glazing system for each of the three experiments. Only in experiment 3 did the large pane fail completely after some twenty minutes exposure to the enclosure fire. Again many factors including the rate of heating, crack edge profile, bifurcation patterns, weight of glass, and edge restraint influence the extent of loss of integrity. Inspection of the gas temperature profiles suggests that a fire in the center of the enclosure produces a steady upper gas layer temperature of between 500°C and 700°C while the corner fire scenario continues to produce a gradual increase in gas temperature over time. Thus, the rate and mode of heating may well influence the behavior of the glazing system. Further, depending on the fire source, the increasing upper gas layer temperature may or may not be associated with an increasing incident flux on the surface of the glass.

The issues that have been raised and briefly discussed in this chapter were the catalyst for the initiation of a program of work to further investigate the behavior of single and double glazing in real fires in full scale rooms.

CONCLUDING REMARKS

1. Many factors, including the location of the fire, severity of the fire, thickness of the glass, glass/frame assembly, geometry of the glazing, and edge quality, influence the propensity of glass to fracture and its subsequent fallout.
2. Total fallout of the large glass pane only occurred in experiment 3 with minimal loss of integrity in the associated small pane.
3. In experiment 3 the upper gas layer temperature profile was characterized by a steady rate of increase to peak temperature, whereas the other two experiments were characterized by upper gas layer temperatures which after the initial growth period approached steady state.
4. All of the panes of glass exhibited similar cracking patterns characterized by the formation of closures, i.e., areas of glass totally bounded by crack fracture.
5. The range of times for the occurrence of the first crack occurring in the large or small panes was 4.1-5.6 minutes. In contrast, the range of times for the occurrence of the second crack was 5.0-12.35 minutes.

6. The location of the fires and the observed behavior of the glazing systems suggest that the mode and rate of heating of the glass will significantly influence the behavior of the glass.

7. The results of these preliminary experiments suggest that in some circumstances an increasing upper gas layer temperature may not always be directly associated with an increasing incident flux on the glass.

8. This work suggests that the behaviors of glazing systems in fire may, for fire safety engineering purposes, by usefully linked to incremental increases in fire severity.

9. Much more work is required in order to develop a fuller understanding of the behaviors of glazing systems in fire and the reliable quantification of such behaviors for use in fire safety engineering.

REFERENCES

1. S. K. S. Hassani, T. J. Shields, and G. W. Silcock, Thermal Fracture of Window Glazing: Performance of Glazing in Fire, *Journal of Applied Fire Science, 4*:4, pp. 249-263, 1994-95.

2. S. K. S. Hassani, T. J. Shields, and G. W. Silcock, In Situ Experimental Thermal Stress Measurements in Glass Subjected to Enclosure Fires, *Journal of Applied Fire Science, 5*:2, pp. 123-134, 1995-96.

CHAPTER 5

The Behavior of Double Glazing in an Enclosure Fire

T. J. Shields, G. W. H. Silcock, and S. K. S. Hassani

Previous work in relation to the behavior of glazing exposed to real fire conditions has largely focused on single panes of glass. This chapter introduces work which focuses on the behaviors of ordinary double glazed units exposed to real fire conditions, with respect to the location of the fire, position of the glazing, and the influence of the descending hot gas layer. The temperature and induced stress fields in the glass, time to first and subsequent cracks, crack bifurcation patterns, and extent of glass fall out are reported and discussed.

It has been shown that the expedient assumptions with respect to catastrophic glass failures in enclosure fires used in simulation modeling or engineering estimations of fire growth are no longer valid or tenable except perhaps in some worst case scenarios. Previous work has established that the thermally induced stresses are responsible for the initial cracking in glazing occurring at the edges of the shaded areas of the glass [1]. Practically all of the experimental work to date with respect to fire has focused on single [2, 3] panes of glass. However, the technology associated with glazing products has advanced considerably such that in many countries multi-pane and low emissivity glazing systems are in common use. This chapter builds on previous work and reports the results of initial investigations into the behaviors of double glazed window units exposed to real fire conditions, with respect to the location of the fire, position of the glazing, and the descending hot gas layer. The temperature and induced stress fields in the glass, time to first and subsequent fractures, crack bifurcation patterns, and extent of glass fall out are also reported and discussed.

EXPERIMENTAL FACILITY

The experimental rig used in the series of investigations was 1.7 m high, 1.5 m wide, and 1.6 m deep, constructed and instrumented as shown in Figure 1. The enclosure walls were 100 mm concrete block work, the roof consisted of 115 mm reinforced concrete with 15 mm thick insulation board fixed to the underside, and the concrete floor was covered with 15 mm thick insulation board. An adjustable vent 1240 mm high × 120 mm wide was provided in one corner of the room with an adjacent tree of thermocouples to measure the inlet and outlet gas temperatures. The fuel source for these experiments consisted of wood cribs mounted on a load cell which could be positioned in a corner or center of the room. The wood crib measured approximately 500 mm × 500 mm × 500 mm and arranged in an eight 30 mm × 30 mm stick high stack with 30 mm spacing. The total mass of the fuel used in each test was approximately 19.0 kg. In order to investigate the effect of the location of the fire, the wood cribs were located in the center and in a corner of the room.

Ordinary 6 mm glass was used in all the window arrangements that were built into the enclosure Figure 1 with temperature compensated strain gauges [2] to

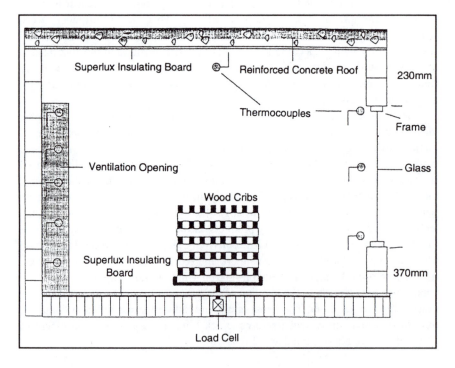

Figure 1. Instrumented experimental room: double glazing experiments.

measure the thermally induced edge strain, Figure 3. Type K sheathed thermo-couples were used to measure gas temperatures within the enclosure, Figure 1 and glazing surface temperatures, Figures 2 and 3. The window arrangement was such that during the tests the small panes were totally immersed in the hot gas layer shortly after the fuel was ignited whereas the tall pane was subjected to a two-zone environment.

Details of the fire location and ventilation employed during the three experi-ments with double glazing are given in Table 1.

RESULTS AND OBSERVATIONS

Summary of Results

The results obtained from these experiments with respect to the occurrence of the first and subsequent cracks and extent of glass fall out are summarized in Table 2.

The double glazing units retained their integrity in each of the three experiments.

The location of cracking times for first, second, and subsequent cracking for the inner leaf of the double glazed systems and crack bifurcations are shown in Figures 4, 5, and 6.

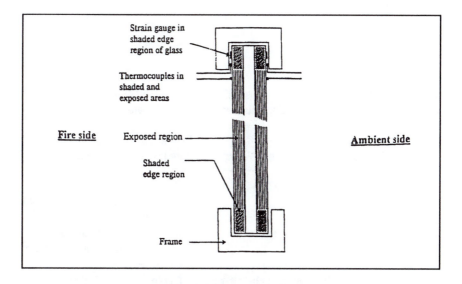

Figure 2. Schematic representation of double glazing showing
arrangement of instruments.

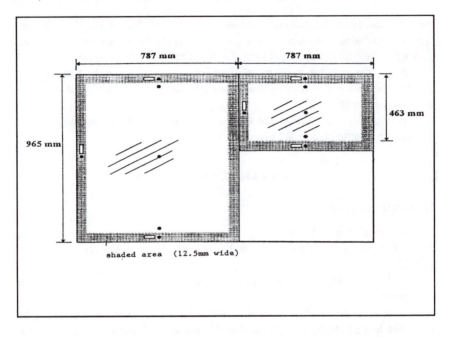

Figure 3. Window arrangement, dimensions, and instrumentation doublesingle glazing.

Table 1. Double Glazing Experiments (6 mm Glass) by Position of Fire in Enclosure and Ventilation Rates

Experiment No.	Type of Glazing	Fire Load Type/Weight	Position of Fire Load	Ventilation Opening
1	Double	Wood crib / 19.1 kg	Corner	Fully open 1240 mm × 120 mm
2	Double	Wood crib / 19.1 kg	Center	Fully open 1240 mm × 120 mm
3	Double	Wood crib / 19.1 kg	Center	Fully open 1050 mm × 83 mm

Table 2. Summary of Results for Double Glazing Exposed
to Real Enclosure Fire Conditions

Experiment No.	Time to 1st Crack (min)				Measured Edge Strain at Cracking (μs)				Time to Loss of Integrity Outer Panes (mins)		% Glass Fall Out Outer Panes	
	Large Pane		Small Pane		Large Pane		Small Pane		Large Pane	Small Pane	Large Pane	Small Pane
	Inner	Outer	Inner	Outer	Inner	Outer	Inner	Outer	Outer	Outer	Outer	Outer
1	5.1	12.7	5.3	14.6	475	340	450	430	—	—	—	—
2	4.9	13.2	4.1	14.0	—	—	—	—	21.0	—	2	—
3	5.2	19.8	5.1	18.8	530	530	—	—	—	—	—	—

Enclosure Gas Temperature Profiles

The enclosure gas temperature profiles at ceiling height and adjacent to the window for the experiments listed in Table 1 are given in Figures 7, 8, and 9.

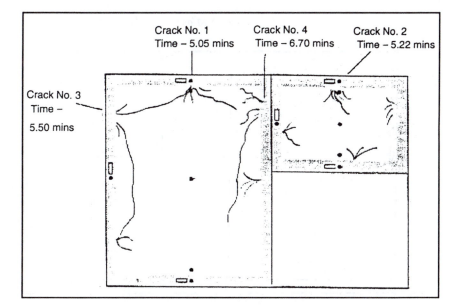

Figure 4. Experiment 1: Double glazing, time, sequence, and location of cracking and crack bifurcation patterns.

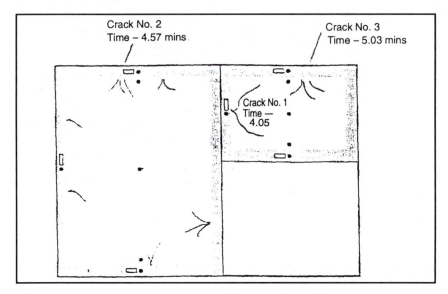

Figure 5. Experiment 2: Double glazing, time, sequence, and location of cracking and crack bifurcation patterns.

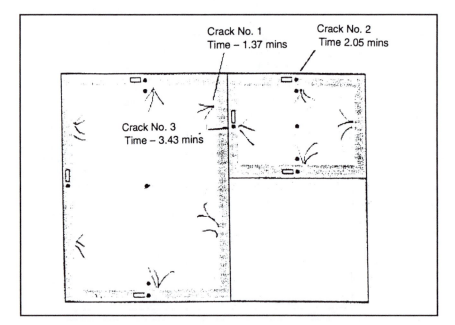

Figure 6. Experiment 3: Double glazing, time, sequence, and location of cracking and crack bifurcation patterns.

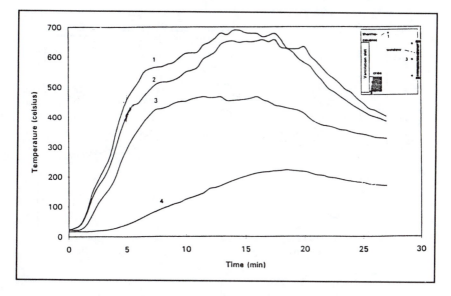

Figure 7. Experiment No. 1: Gas temperature profile in
the fire enclosure.

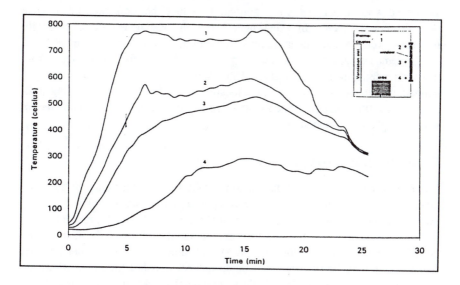

Figure 8. Experiment No. 2: Gas temperature profile in
the fire enclosure.

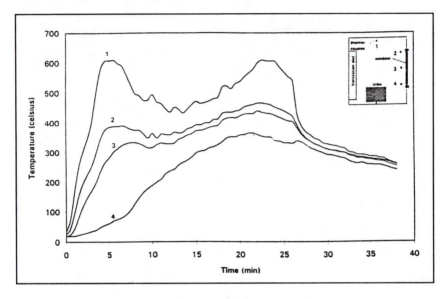

Figure 9. Experiment No. 3: Gas temperature profile
in the fire enclosure.

It would appear that the effect of the induced upper gas layer flow patterns associated with corner fire is to significantly reduce the temperature difference over the hot gas layer. In experiment No. 1 the gas temperatures gradually increased over the first fifteen minutes of the burn, whereas in experiment No. 2 the gas temperatures increased more rapidly over the first five minutes and from thereon tended toward steady state. Thus, taking into account the relevant gas temperatures in experiment No. 3, the location of the fire, and size of vents used, it is clear that the location of the fire and size of the vents influence the manner in which the glazing is heated up.

Exposed Surface Temperatures

In experiments No. 2 and 3, the location of the fire is in the center of the room whereas in experiment No. 1 the fire is located in a corner approximately 1 m away from the glazing. From inspection of Figures 10, 11, and 12, it will be seen that in the early stages of fire development the middle section of the glazing may be hotter than the top section, indicating that radiation from the fuel bed and flame plume may be the dominant mode of heat transfer. Similar patterns are apparent for the small panes of glass, Figures 13, 14, and 15, although the temperature differences over the depth of the glazing are smaller than those recorded for the large panes.

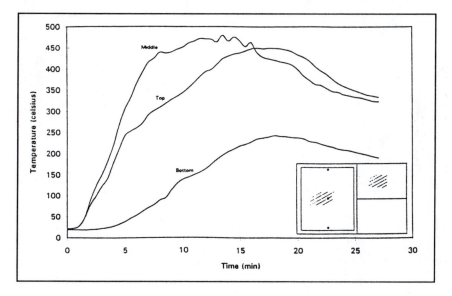

Figure 10. Experiment No. 1: Exposed surface temperature:
large inner glass pane.

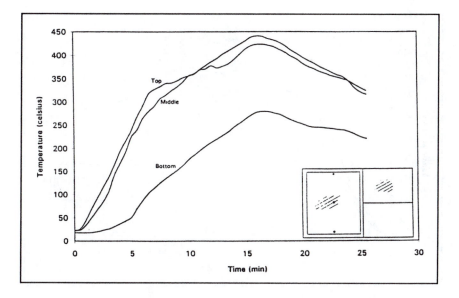

Figure 11. Experiment No. 2: Exposed surface temperature:
large inner glass pane.

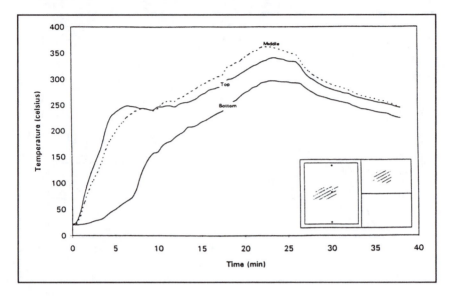

Figure 12. Experiment No. 3: Exposed surface temperature:
large inner glass pane.

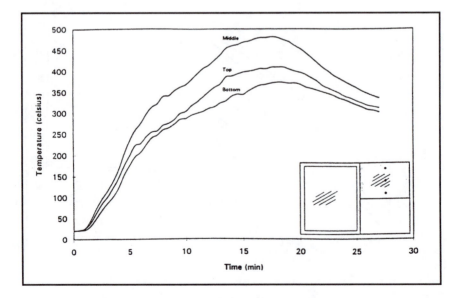

Figure 13. Experiment No. 1: Exposed surface temperature:
small inner glass pane.

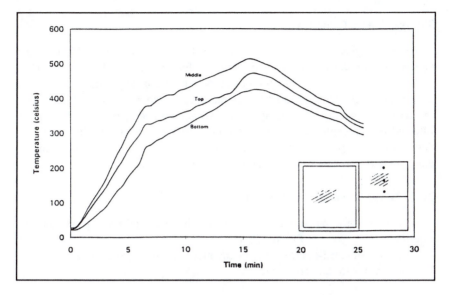

Figure 14. Experiment No. 2: Exposed surface temperature:
small inner glass pane.

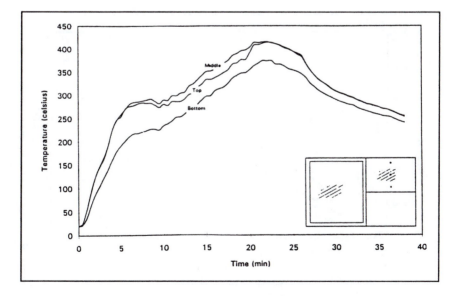

Figure 15. Experiment No. 3: Exposed surface temperature:
small inner glass pane.

Shaded Glass Temperatures

The shaded glass temperatures recorded at the locations given in Figure 3 for the large and small glass panes are presented in Figures 16, 17, 18, 19, 20, and 21.

The shaded glass edge temperatures recorded for the large inner glass panes correspond to gas temperature profiles recorded in the respective experiments. The maximum shaded glass temperatures were recorded at the top of the pane followed by the center and lower recording locations. However, for the small glass panes, this pattern is not repeated in experiments 1 and 3, although the temperature differences over the depth of the pane are small.

Outer Glass Surface Temperature

The glass surface temperatures recorded for the large and small glass panes in experiment 3 are given in Figures 22 and 23.

The temperature differences over the depth of the glass panes is as intuitively expected greater for the large pane.

Shaded Glass Temperature of Outer Panes

The shaded glass temperatures recorded at the locations shown in Figure 3 for experiment No. 3 are presented in Figures 24 and 25.

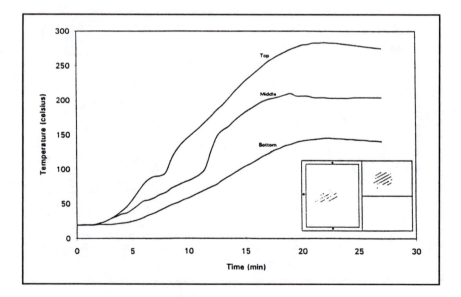

Figure 16. Experiment No. 1: Shaded edge temperatures:
large inner glass pane.

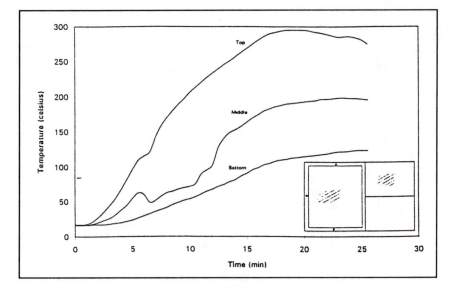

Figure 17. Experiment No. 2: Shaded edge temperatures:
large inner glass pane.

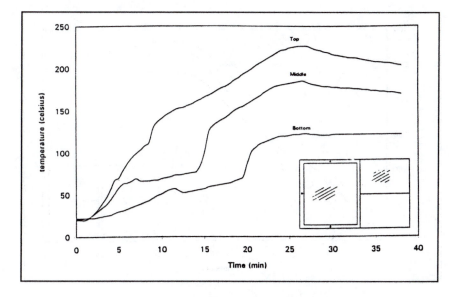

Figure 18. Experiment No. 3: Shaded edge temperatures:
large inner glass pane.

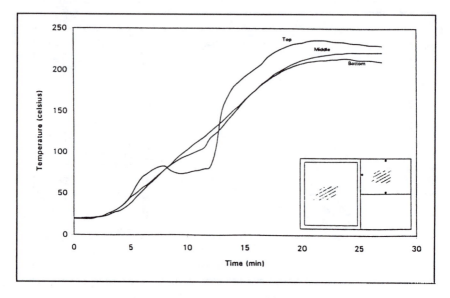

Figure 19. Experiment No. 1: Shaded edge temperatures: small inner glass pane.

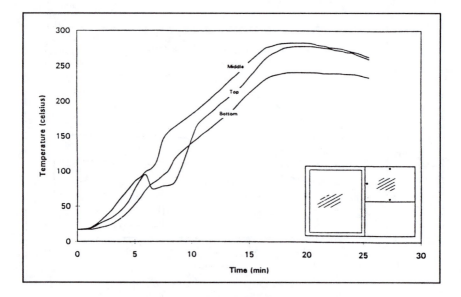

Figure 20. Experiment No. 2: Shaded edge temperatures: small inner glass pane.

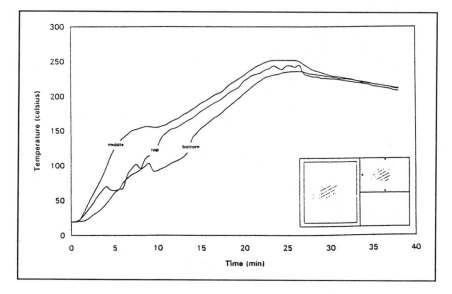

Figure 21. Experiment No. 3: Shaded edge temperatures:
small inner glass pane.

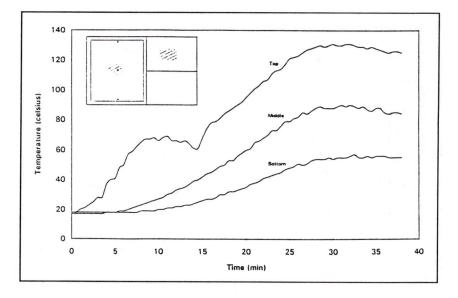

Figure 22. Exposed surface temperatures:
large outer glass pane.

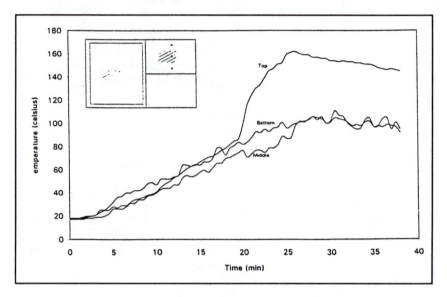

Figure 23. Exposed surface temperature:
small outer glass pane.

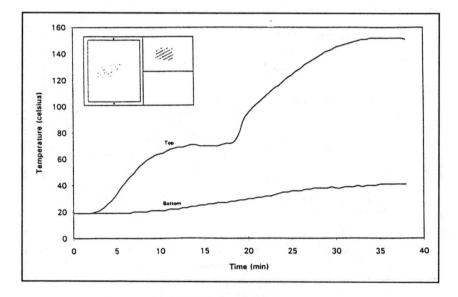

Figure 24. Shaded edge temperature:
large outer glass pane.

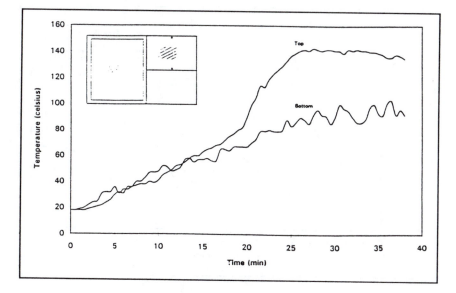

Figure 25. Shaded edge temperatures:
small outer glass pane.

The maximum shaded glass temperature for the large and small panes was approximately 140°C.

Thermally Induced Strains

The thermally induced strains recorded in experiments No. 1 and 3 are given in Figures 26 and 27.

The differences in the magnitude of the measured edge strains between the small and large pane and between the inner and outer panes will be noted.

ANALYSIS OF RESULTS

The times for the first and subsequent cracks for the large and small panes are given in Table 2. Practically all the first cracks in the inner panes occurred five minutes into the experiments. Interestingly, although at five minutes into the burns the upper gas layer temperatures are significantly different, the gas temperatures measured adjacent to the areas where cracking occurred were similar, i.e., approximately 400°C. The first cracks in the outer panes occurred at between thirteen minutes and twenty minutes into the experiments. It would appear that the rate and/or duration of heating influences the time to occurrence of first cracking in the outer glass panes. The recorded strains for the large and

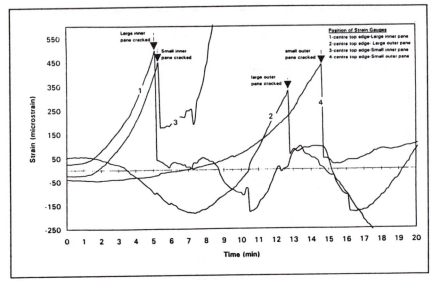

Figure 26. Strains vs. time for large and small
double glazing unit.

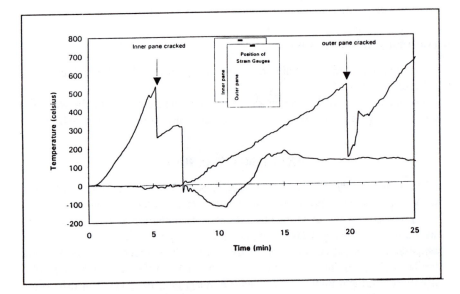

Figure 27. Strains vs. time for large double glazing unit.

small inner panes at the time of occurrence of the first cracks were between 530 and 430 micro strains. The temperature difference, i.e., between the glass surface temperature and shaded edge temperature for the top edges of the large and small panes was approximately 160°C.

Examination of Figures 10 through 15 indicate that the middle sections of the panes of glass were hotter than the top sections of the panes during early stages of the experiments. Given timber cribs as fuel and the distance of the fuel bed from the glazing radiation was the mode of heating. Consequently, due to in-depth absorption of radiation the middle sections of the glass achieved higher temperatures early on in the experiments.

The extent of cracking in the outer panes is illustrated in Figures 4, 5, and 6, and the times to the occurrence of first cracks are given in Table 2. Significantly, the outer panes of the double glazing although considerably weakened, remained in situ with negligible loss of integrity.

CONCLUDING REMARKS

Many factors influence the propensity for glass to fracture and subsequently fail.

In the set of experiments reported, the outer panes, although considerably weakened, retained their integrity.

All of the outer panes exhibited similar cracking patterns with first cracking occurring between thirteen to twenty minutes into the experiments.

The results of these preliminary experiments suggest double glazing units will remain in situ in fire longer than is currently anticipated and that failure of such systems can be related to fire severity.

Much more work is required to develop a fuller understanding of the behavior of double glazing systems, particularly low emissivity glazing units, in order to produce reliable engineering data for use in fire safety engineering.

REFERENCES

1. S. K. S. Hassani, T. J. Shields, and G. W. Silcock, Thermal Fracture of Window Glazing: Performance of Glazing in Fire, *Journal of Applied Fire Science, 4*:4, 1995-1995.
2. S. K. S. Hassani, J. Shields, and G. W. Silcock, An Experimental Investigation into the Behaviour of Glazing in Enclosure Fires, *Journal of Applied Fire Science, 4*:4, 1994-1995.
3. S. K. S. Hassani, T. J. Shields, and G. W. Silcock, In Situ Experimental Thermal Stress Measurements in Glass Subjected to Enclosure Fires, *Journal of Applied Fire Science, 4*:4, 1994-1995.

CHAPTER 6

History and Use of Wired Glass in Fire Rated Applications

Donald W. Belles

This chapter provides background information for the use of 1/4-in. thick polished wired glass. It reviews the effects of existing fire and building code provisions and the federal safety glazing regulations of the Consumer Product Safety Commission (CPSC) on the use of wired glass. It discusses a "loophole" in the codes that provokes proposals to use twenty-minute fire rated glazings (tested without hose stream) in one-hour partitions separating exit access corridors, potentially jeopardizing those separations. The information for this chapter comes from published sources, and from the Flat Glass Manufacturers Association of Japan and Pilkington Glass Limited for whom the author serves as consultant.

Fire rated glazings have a number of physical attributes designed to enhance building security and safety. For example, glazings in doors help avoid accidents by allowing persons to see through the doors. In parking structures, glazed exit enclosures provide fire separation while relieving personal security problems. In exterior walls, fire rated glazings allow light to enter, but still provide protection against external exposures. However, architects, specifying engineers, and building officials should understand the limitations as well as the advantages of such unique products.

Wired glass was invented in the mid-1800s for use as "fireproof and burglar-proof glass." Wired glass has been used successfully in fire rated applications for more than 100 years [1-3]. Until the last several years, 1/4-in. thick, polished, wired glass has been the only fire rated glazing commercially available. Now, a variety of fire rated glazings are offered for sale in the United States. Most of the new products are clear (non-wire) glazings and claim to have fire protection ratings ranging from twenty to ninety minutes. They consist of monolithic borosilicate or calcium-silica tempered glass, special heat-absorbing materials sandwiched between two tempered lites, ceramic glazing, and special interlayer laminated products. A twenty-minute fire rated laminated glass product with wires in the interlayer also has recently been introduced. The new fire rated glazings have a variety of performance characteristics. Sales efforts to gain market share have given rise to claims and counterclaims on product behavior, limitations, and suitability. Questions related to human impact and lacerative injuries have been raised. Fire protection performance has been challenged on the basis of the ability of glazings to:

- serve as fire rated barriers
- protect openings in fire rated barriers
- resist radiant heat transfer
- resist thermal shock
- resist the impact, cooling, and erosion effects of a hose stream

Because of the many different types of fire rated glazings now offered in the market place, each with unique qualities and performance characteristics, the ability to identify products after installation takes on greater importance. Glazings must be identifiable in order to verify the products are used within the conditions of their third-party approval or listing. Glazings installed in fire rated barriers must be capable of maintaining the integrity of the barrier. Additionally, glazings used within the barriers at locations subject to human impact also must meet applicable safety glazing standards.

Polished wired glass of minimum 1/4-in. thickness is routinely specified for the protection of openings in fire rated partitions and in the fire rated doors. Wired glass is favored because it enjoys five distinct advantages over other fire rated glazings, namely:

1. Wired glass is easily cut to size in the field to fit an opening and thus satisfies the replacement market;
2. Wired glass meets *both* safety glazing and fire protection requirements of the U.S. model building codes and all known building codes;
3. Wired glass may be purchased from local sources and installed, or replaced if broken, very quickly, often within hours;
4. Wired glass is ten to twenty-five times less expensive than alternate fire rated glazings; and
5. Wired glass's unique mesh construction provides a visual warning that diminishes inadvertent human contact with the glazing.

Safety glazing requirements have two principal sources. They are found in the federal regulations of the Consumer Product Safety Commission, published at 16 CFR 1201, and in model building codes. How the CPSC regulations and the building code limitations interrelate is often confusing and is discussed in later sections of this chapter. Additional questions arise as to how fire rated glazings are to be qualified for use. That is, which fire tests are required for what applications?

When is the hose stream test required? What limitations exist on the size and number of lites permitted—for example, in a one-hour partition separating an exit access corridor? These, too, are discussed below.

MANUFACTURING WIRED GLASS

There are two major production processes for polished wired glass. One is the two-stage process invented by Pilkington Glass, the U.K. supplier, and the other is the continuous production of "Duplex" process. The processes vary slightly from manufacturer to manufacturer, but in both processes, at the end of the furnace, wire mesh is embedded in hot molten glass at the proper glass thickness, and the formed glass ribbon subsequently travels into a cooling zone for annealing. In the two-stage process, the glass ribbon is then cut into large sheets for subsequent grinding and polishing to remove surface irregularities. In the Duplex process, the glass ribbon is continuously ground, polished, washed, and then cut into large sheets.

Wired glass is shipped to the United States in case lots using intermodal containers. Stock sheets are approximately 50 square feet in surface area with approximately 1,500 to 1,200 square feet of glass per case.

The final thickness of the polished wired glass also varies slightly from manufacturer to manufacturer, but all such glass is within the specifications and tolerances contained in ASTM C1036-91, "Standard Specification for Flat Glass." Wire mesh is No. 24 BS gauge (0.020 in. ± 0.002 in.) mild steel. Where the wires intersect, they must be welded. The wire mesh is centered ±1/16 in. between the two surfaces of the glass. This means the mesh has a minimum cover of 1/16-in. of glass.

All 1/4-in. polished wired glass distributed in the United States is manufactured under factory follow-up service and qualifies for use in fire rated barriers. All 1/4-in. polished wired glass is eligible for labeling [4].

FIRE TESTING WIRED GLASS

When wired glass is exposed to fire in accordance with standard fire tests for window assemblies [5-7], the glass cracks within minutes, but the wire mesh prevents openings. At about 1,600°F, the glass starts to become viscous and slumps out of the opening if exposure at this or higher temperatures continues [8]. During standard fire endurance testing, furnace temperatures exceed 1,600°F at approximately forty-five minutes. If wired glass is to withstand a fire exposure of forty-five-minutes without slumping out of the frame, the glass must be securely held in a listed frame. In terms of performance in actual fires, wired glass behavior is temperature dependent. In other words, wired glass remains in place indefinitely if not heated above 1,550-1,600°F.

Wired glass materially thinner than 1/4-in. or with wires running in one direction may not pass the forty-five-minute fire test. The wire mesh pattern may be square, rectangular, diamond shaped or even hexagonal, but the diamond pattern is the type predominantly distributed in the United States. As noted, the wires must be welded together at intersections, and the wire mesh must be "buried" in the glass with a minimum 1/16-in. covering.

Fire rated glazings, such as wired glass, have traditionally been evaluated by *both* a forty-five-minute fire exposure and hose stream application. The hose stream is used following the fire exposure because fire barriers are subjected to exposures other than heat from a fire. For example, during the course of a fire, impact from overturning furniture, collapsing piles of storage, falling debris, pressure waves created by minor explosions, or impact and thermal shock resulting from application of hose streams could affect the performance of a fire barrier. The fire hose stream test serves two purposes—a means of simulating objects impacting glazing during a fire and a means of evaluating the effects of sudden cooling or thermal shock on the glazing system.

SBC AND FIRE PROTECTION RATED GLAZING

Fire protection rated glazings are principally used in exterior walls, in fire rated doors, and in one-hour partitions separating exit access corridors. The 1994 edition of the Standard Building Code ("SBC"), Table 700, expressly requires glazing in exterior walls to have a minimum three-quarter-hour fire protection rating. Fire windows in exterior walls must be qualified by tests conducted in accordance with ASTM E163 [7]. See SBC Paragraph 705.1.3.2. ASTM E163 states the method is "intended to evaluate the ability of a window or other light-transmitting assembly to remain in an opening during a predetermined test exposure of 45-minute duration." Therefore, the SBC requires fire protection rated glazing in exterior walls to be tested in accordance with ASTM E163 and to achieve a forty-five-minute fire protection rating when subjected to *both* fire endurance and hose stream tests. The SBC does not contain specific limits for the maximum area or maximum dimensions for fire windows in exterior walls. However, the SBC, Paragraph 705.1.3.1 reference to NFPA 80 [9] might be interpreted to set such limits. See NFPA 80, Section 13-3.

Table 700 requires partitions separating exit access corridors to have a minimum fire resistance rating of one hour using opening protectives with minimum twenty-minute fire protection rating. The Table 700 opening protective criteria are apparently developed with fire doors in mind.

SBC Paragraphs 704.2.1.4 and 705.1.3.2 set criteria for the use of fire protection rated "view panels" in one-hour partitions. Paragraph 704.2.1.4 is prescriptive in nature, setting parameters for labeled wired glass and labeled glass block assemblies. Individual wired glass lites are limited to a maximum of 1296 square inches, whereas glass block assemblies are limited to a maximum of

120 square feet. Neither wired glass nor glass block may exceed 25 percent of the wall area separating each space from the exit access corridor. View panels of wired glass, glass block, and other types of fire protection rated glazing, like windows in exterior walls, must be qualified by tests conducted in accordance with ASTM E163. See Paragraph 705.1.3.2. This means fire protection rated glazing used as view panels in one hour partitions must withstand a forty-five-minute fire endurance test plus hose stream test in accordance with ASTM E163.

The SBC does not contain specific area or individual lite size limits for fire protection rated glazing other than wired glass and glass block. Individual lites of other than wired glass or glass block should be limited to the maximum size successfully tested. Maximum area limits for "other" fire protection rated glazings might vary, depending upon the characteristics of the particular glazing.

Fire protection rated glazing used in fire doors is regulated by Paragraphs 705.1.3.2, 705.1.3.6, and Table 705.1.3.6. Fire doors must be qualified by tests conducted in accordance with ASTM E152 [10] which would ordinarily include fire endurance and hose stream tests. The historical practice for the use of wired glass in fire doors has been to test one door with a 1/4 in. thick, polished wired glass panel. Assuming satisfactory performance, any 1/4 in. thick, polished wired glass complying with ASTM E163 is permitted to be used in the fire door. Fire protection rated glazings, other than wired glass, are so dissimilar that each glazing must be evaluated with each fire door. Area limits are set for wired glass in Table 705.1.3.6. Fire protection rated glazing, other than wired glass, is limited to the maximum size successfully tested.

The Standard Building Code, Paragraph 705.1.3.2.2 requires twenty-minute fire protection rated doors, used to protect openings in one hour partitions, to be tested in accordance with ASTM E152 without hose stream test. The hose stream exemption for twenty-minute fire doors is based upon historical precedent. Years ago, the SBC required 1-3/4 in. thick, solid core, wood doors to protect openings in one-hour corridor partitions. Solid core wood doors had been proven adequate by experience. Subsequent efforts to make the SBC more performance oriented resulted in deleting the 1-3/4 in., solid core, wood verbiage. A performance based requirement—twenty-minute assembly—was substituted. Although 1-3/4 in. thick solid core wood doors generally will achieve a twenty-minute rating, many would fail ASTM E152 if the hose stream is applied after the twenty-minute fire exposure. Since the performance of 1-3/4 in. thick wood doors was judged adequate by experience, Paragraph 705.1.3.2.2 was developed to allow the continued use of these doors.

TWENTY-MINUTE RATED GLAZING

A number of twenty-minute rated glazings, listed without hose stream, are being marketed in the United States. Producers and distributors of fire rated glazings sometimes cite the 705.1.3.2.2 hose stream exemption for fire doors to justify the use of fire protection rated glazing tested for twenty-minute fire endurance without application of the hose stream. The logic is facially appealing. For example, suppose a fabricated glass door is proposed for use in place of the traditional 1-3/4 in. thick solid core wood door. Shouldn't the performance requirements for the glass door be the same as those for the wood door? Suppose a door assembly is to be tested, and the assembly incorporates glazing in sidelights and/or a transom. Why should the glazing in the sidelights and/or transom adjacent to the door, tested as a part of the door assembly, be subject to different requirements?

Despite the apparent logic, material differences in performance between twenty-minute fire protection rated glazings and 1-3/4 in. solid wood doors warrant different treatment. The performance of the doors is well documented through fire tests, full scale fire experiments and actual experience [11-13]. Wood doors are inherently durable and not subject to thermal shock. In contrast, fire protection rated glazings may break out of the frame when impacted by falling objects. Glazing may also fail after being heated in a fire when exposed to water from a failed water line, an operating sprinkler head, or the fire department's hose stream [14]. If the glazing fails during a fire, smoke and heat could spread to exit access corridors preventing escape of building occupants. If twenty-minute fire protection rated glazing (without evaluation by hose stream) is used to protect openings in one-hour corridor partitions, safety margins may be compromised and lives endangered.

FIRE TESTS OF TWENTY-MINUTE GLAZING

The performance of a 1/4-in. thick, twenty-minute fire rated, listed (without hose stream) glazing was evaluated during a series of six tests conducted recently at a nationally recognized independent laboratory [15]. The tests were designed principally to determine if a twenty-minute fire rated glazing material would remain in the frame during the fire endurance test described in ASTM E163 when the glazing is exposed to a small water spray applied periodically during the test.

In these tests, six identical listed twenty-minute fire rated glazing specimens, 34 in. by 32 in. by 1/4 in. thick, were tested. In five of the tests, glazing was mounted in a gypsum board partition in a listed steel fire window frame. The entire assembly was fabricated in a test frame approximately 50 in. by 50 in. The test frame design and glass installation was undertaken by the test laboratory and in accordance with the manufacturer's published directions. Each test specimen was placed in front of a fire resistance furnace (see Figure 1). In four of five tests, the laboratory controlled the furnace interior temperature to ensure the furnace time-temperature conditions corresponded to the standard time-temperatures

Figure 1. Each test specimen was placed in front of
a fire resistance furnace.

specified in ASTM E163. In one of the five tests, the temperature in the furnace
was raised slower than standard. Also, in one of the five tests, glazing was loosely
mounted to reduce stresses on the glass due to warping of the frame. A sixth test
was conducted with a specimen mounted in a wood stud and gypsum board
partition with the lite installed in a wood surround with a minimum 1/4-in.
clearance along all sides, top and bottom. The specimen mounting was purposely
constructed to prevent imposing any stresses on the glass due to warping of
the frame.

As noted, all fire rated glazing specimens were listed for twenty-minute applications without evaluation by a hose stream. The principal purpose of these six tests
was to determine whether the twenty-minute fire rated glazing would withstand an
exposure to a small water spray applied periodically during fire endurance tests.
During the fire exposure, the test procedure called for spraying water every two
and one-half minutes for a duration of ten seconds. The procedure involved
directing the water onto the unexposed surface of the glazing near the top of the
lite through a spray nozzle located twenty-four inches from, and perpendicular to,
the glazing with the long axis of the spray pattern positioned vertically. The nozzle
was adjusted for a water flow rate of 1/2 gallon per minute. Water was to be
sprayed over an area roughly the size of a football on the unexposed surface of the

glass in a pattern that had a long (vertical) axis of approximately twelve inches and a short axis of approximately five inches.

The test parameters assumed the twenty-minute fire rated glazing would resist the fire endurance exposure without difficulty in accordance with its listing; however, that premise turned out to be incorrect. In three of the tests, the glazing failed prior to the first application of water, scheduled for two minutes, thirty seconds. Even in the experiment employing the special wood frame construction to avoid warpage forces on the glass, the glass shattered into small fragments and evacuated the opening at one minute, fifty-nine seconds. In the remaining three tests, the glazing shattered shortly after application of the initial spray of water. In all six tests the glazing shattered prior to five minutes leaving an approximately 900 square inch unprotected opening (see Figure 2).

These tests strongly suggest there may be little or no safety margin when twenty-minute fire protection rated glazing, tested without the hose stream, is permitted in interior fire rated partitions. The fragile nature of this glazing, compared to 1-3/4 in. solid core wood doors, argues for evaluating the glazing for thermal shock and impact resistance as an integral part of fire testing. A fire endurance of 3/4-hour should be maintained as the minimum acceptable performance for all glazing used in fire rated applications.

Figure 2. Glazing shattered prior to five minutes leaving an approximately 900 square inch unprotected opening.

SAFETY GLAZING CONCERNS

Fire rated glazing materials installed in so-called "hazardous locations" are subject to human impact and therefore must meet safety glazing standards. Prior to the 1982 edition, the SBC simply required glass in defined hazardous locations to comply with ANSI Z97.1, Performance Specifications and Methods of Test for Transparent Safety Glazing Material Used in Buildings. The 1982 edition of the SBC incorporated substantial revisions in the chapter regulating glazing, adding the safety glazing regulations of the federal government, specifically those the Consumer Products Safety Commission (CPSC) adopted and published in 16 CFR 1201. Today, the safety glazing standards consist of the CPSC regulations (16 CFR 1201) in combination with SBC Chapter 24. The interrelationship between the CPSC-mandated test standard (16 CFR 1201), which is similar to, but has distinct differences from, ANSI Z97.1 still leads to confusion.

The CPSC standard applies only to storm doors, combination doors, entrance doors, bathtub and shower doors and enclosures, and patio-type sliding glass doors. The CPSC regulations specifically exempt polished wired glass from 16 CFR 1201 tests when used in doors or other assemblies "to retard the passage of fire where such door or assembly is required by a Federal, state, local, or municipal fire ordinance." Conversely, wired glass used in non-fire rated door applications remains subject to CPSC regulation. The type of glass used in fixed glazed panels, including sidelights, is not covered by 16 CFR 1201 and is, therefore, exempt from CPSC regulations. Glazing exempted from CPSC regulation, including glass in panels adjacent to doors and in partitions, is regulated solely on the basis of the model codes. Chapter 24 of the SBC regulates wired glass irrespective of whether it is used for fire protection purposes.

Products subject to CPSC regulations and products subject to SBC Chapter 24 generally require impact testing in accordance with 16 CFR 1201. Chapter 24 includes a special provision for certain applications of polished wired glass, permitting use of polished wired glass if it complies with ANSI Z97.1. Both 16 CFR 1201 and ANSI Z97.1 specify testing a 34 in. × 76 in. glass specimen clamped in a frame and impacted with a leather punching bag filled with 100 pounds of lead shot (see Figure 3). 16 CFR 1201 allows glazing of 9 square feet or less in surface area to be used in storm and combination doors and fixed panels if it performs adequately when impacted with the 100-pound punching bag dropped from a height of 18 inches, generating 150 ft.-lbs. of energy. In greater sizes and in other hazardous locations, the required impact drop height is 48 inches, generating 400 ft.-lbs. of energy. The ANSI and CPSC test standards are essentially the same in terms of apparatus and interpretation of results when the glazing specimens break. However, ANSI Z97.1 requires impacting the test specimen with the punching bag from an initial drop height of 12 inches, generating 100 ft.-lbs. of energy. If no breakage occurs, the specimen is again impacted, but

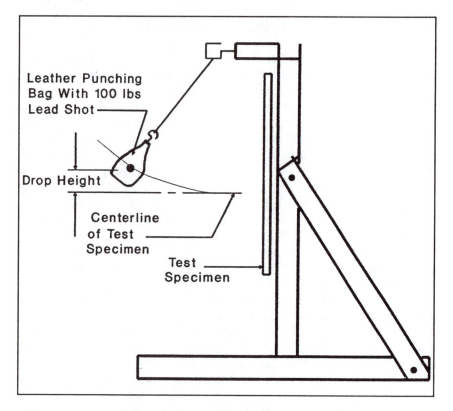

Figure 3. Schematic of test apparatus—ANSI Z97.1.

this time at a drop height of 18 inches. If no breakage occurs, the specimen is again impacted from a drop height of 48 inches. Regardless of whether the CPSC or ANSI standard is followed, the interpretation of the impact results is the same. A product is judged to perform satisfactorily (i.e., it passes) if, when breakage first occurs (and even though numerous cracks and fissures may appear), a 3-in. diameter sphere does not pass freely through any opening in the test specimen. If the glass disintegrates, as in the case of tempered glass, there is a "pass" when the ten largest crack-free particles selected five minutes after the tests weigh no more than the weight of 10 square inches of the original specimen. If the specimen remains intact after the 48-in. drop test, performance is judged satisfactory.

In summary, CPSC regulations exempt polished wired glass in fire rated applications from the safety glazing requirements of 16 CFR 1201. However, Chapter 24 of the SBC requires 1/4-in. polished wired glass, used in fire doors and the defined fixed glazed panels, to meet the test requirements of ANSI Z97.1. For many years, all four wired glass manufacturers have self-certified that their 1/4-in.

polished wired glass met the safety glazing requirements of ANSI Z97.1—and therefore the requirements of SBC Chapter 24. All four manufacturers recently subjected their 1/4-in. polished wired glass to independent testing by nationally recognized U.S. laboratories to verify compliance with ANSI Z97.1. Independent labs verified that all four manufacturers' 1/4-in. polished wire glass meets the safety glazing requirements of ANSI Z97.1 [16-20]. The four manufacturers continue to verify production compliance with periodic impact testing.

It must be emphasized that ANSI Z97.1 and 16 CFR 1201 do *not* require any glazing material to resist breaking at the impact levels tested. Instead, those standards state that, when the glass specimens do break, the glazing must break in a relatively safe pattern. The satisfactory (safe) breakage patterns are described in detail in the test methods of each standard. Polished wired glass passes the ANSI Z97.1 because, when impacted at 100 ft.-lbs., it breaks in compliance with the satisfactory patterns specified in that standard. The satisfactory break patterns are defined in the standard so as to recognize a minimal risk of injury when the glass breaks "safely."

The CPSC was recently petitioned to eliminate the exemption for polished wired glass in 16 CFR 1201 and to expand the definition of covered glazing materials to include transparent ceramics [21]. The CPSC examined all available evidence and denied the petition, concluding that "information is not now available to establish that either noncomplying wired glass in fire doors nor noncomplying transparent ceramics in any of the products subject to the standard present an unreasonable risk of injury" [22]. In reaching this conclusion, the CPSC examined the evidence of glass injuries the petitioner submitted and that contained in the National Electronic Injury Surveillance System ("NEISS") data base to identify and evaluate any injuries associated with wired glass. From January 1, 1985 through November 30, 1992, the CPSC identified a total of seven reports of injuries requiring treatment associated with wired glass. On the basis of the injury reports, the CPSC estimated that approximately thirty-five injuries a year are associated with wired glass requiring hospital treatment. The injuries resulted in an average cost of treatment of about $3,400. In contrast, eliminating the wired glass exemption would, according to the CPSC, result in a total cost of more than $36,000,000 a year.

SUMMARY

Polished wired glass, 1/4-in. thick, has been used in the United States for more than 100 years. Millions of square feet are installed each year. Experience from a safety glazing standpoint can be characterized as reasonable. Wired glass used in locations subject to human impact has been evaluated in compliance with ANSI Z97.1 for many years. Injuries, in terms of frequency and severity, have been relatively minor. Wired glass differs from other types of glazing in that the wire mesh makes the glass highly visible, reducing the probability of inadvertent human impact. A combination of the visibility of the product and compliance with ANSI Z97.1 may account for the favorable injury experience.

Polished wired glass is able to resist a standard fire exposure for forty-five minutes. Wired glass is also able to resist the cooling and impact of a hose stream applied immediately after the forty-five-minute fire endurance test. To perform as expected, the wired glass must be securely held in a listed steel frame.

Historically, fire rated glazing in one-hour partitions has been required to achieve a minimum forty-five-minute fire protection rating, resisting *both* the fire endurance and hose stream tests prescribed by ASTM E163. On the other hand, twenty-minute doors (1-3/4-in. wood solid core doors) protecting corridor door openings are exempted from the hose stream test by SBC, Paragraph 705.1.3.2.2. Some distributors reference Paragraph 705.1.3.2.2 to justify the use of twenty-minute fire protection rated glazing (tested without hose stream) in one-hour corridor partitions.

The use of twenty-minute glazings (tested without hose stream) in one-hour corridor partitions may jeopardize exit access corridor separation. Glazing is fragile in comparison to wood doors. During fire, falling objects may impact the glazing or the glass may be heated and then shocked by water spraying from a failed water line. Mechanical impact or thermal shock may break the glass allowing smoke and heat to spread to exit access routes.

REFERENCES

1. *Fire Exposure Tests of Fire Windows*, Underwriters Laboratories, Bulletin of Research No. 28, March 1943.
2. *Fire Tests Nos. 197 a, b, c, July 22, 1914*, Official Reports of the British Fire Prevention Committee, London, 1914.
3. *Fire Tests No. 198 d, e, f, July 22, 1914*, Official Reports of the British Fire Prevention Committee, London, 1914.
4. *Underwriters Laboratories*, Building Materials Directory, pp. 414-418, 1993.
5. *Standard for Fire Tests of Window Assemblies, UL 9* (5th Edition), Underwriters Laboratories, Inc., Northbrook, Illinois, 1989.
6. *Standard for Fire Tests of Window Assemblies, NFPA 257-1990*, National Fire Protection Association, Quincy, Massachusetts, 1990.
7. *Standard Methods of Fire Tests of Window Assemblies, ASTM E 163-84*, American Society for Testing and Materials, Philadelphia, Pennsylvania, 1984.
8. *Fire Protection Handbook* (17th Edition), National Fire Protection Association, Quincy, Massachusetts, pp. 6-87, 1991.
9. *Standard for Fire Doors and Fire Windows, NFPA 80-1992*, National Fire Protection Association, Quincy, Massachusetts, 1992.
10. *Standard Methods of Fire Tests of Door Assemblies, ASTM E 152-81a*, American Society for Testing and Materials, Philadelphia, Pennsylvania, 1981.
11. V. P. Miniutti, Fire Resistance Tests of Solid Wood Flush Doors, *Forest Products Journal, III*:4, Forest Products Research Society, Madison, Wisconsin, April 1958.

12. H. W. Eickner, Fire Resistance of Solid-Core Wood Flush Doors, *Forest Products Journal, 23*:4, Forest Product Laboratory, Madison, Wisconsin, April 1973.

13. W. T. Pacchetti, R. E. Bishop, and A. E. Hole, Project Corridor, Fire and Life Safety Research, *Western Fire Journal*, Office of the California State Fire Marshal, 1974.

14. D. Beason, Fire Endurance of Sprinklered Glass Walls, *Fire Journal*, National Fire Protection Association, Quincy, Massachusetts, pp. 43-45, 79, July 1986.

15. *Small Scale Fire Resistance Testing of Glazing with Water Application—1/4" Thick 20 Minute Fire Rated Glazing, Project No. 12890-97201*, Omega Point Laboratories, August 18, 1994.

16. Miami Testing Laboratory, Inc., *File Number 93-1191, Report No. 1, L-46577*, August 18, 1993.

17. Miami Testing Laboratory, Inc., *File Number 93-1191, Report Number 2, L-46594*, September 1, 1993.

18. ETL Testing Laboratories, Inc., *Report No. 532042*, October 11, 1993.

19. Miami Testing Laboratory, Inc., *File Number 94-579, Report No. 3, L-47057 and Report No. 4, L-47058*, March 28, 1994.

20. Pacific Inspection and Research Laboratory, Inc., *File Nos. 93-374 and 93-375*, December 10, 1993.

21. *CPSC Petition 92-1, Petition of O'Keeffe's Inc. to Amend 16 CFR 1201.2(a)(10) and (11) and Revoke 1201.1(c)(1)*, Safety Standard for Architectural Glazing Materials, 1992.

22. *CPSC letter dated July 22, 1994, by Sadye E. Dunn, Secretary, CPSC, to Kathy D. Steel*, Fox and Grove, San Francisco, California, 1994.

CHAPTER 7

Loose-Fill Cellulose Insulation— An Aging Problem

Donald W. Belles

Loose-fill cellulose insulation consists principally of ground-up newspaper and chemicals. Ground-up newspaper will burn and spread flames. A variety of chemicals are used with cellulose insulation to address the hazards of fire. However, research findings, extending over more than eight years [1-5], indicate the chemical load reduces with time and the performance of fire retardant treated cellulose insulation deteriorates with age.

Fires have been reported as having been spread by, or rekindled in, cellulose insulation. Several such fires in the State of Maryland led to a special "alert" bulletin by the office of the State Fire Marshal [6].

Because of adverse experience, questionable product performance claims and concerns about aging characteristics, Donald W. Belles and Associates, Inc. were requested to study the flammability performance of cellulose insulation. The study involved a literature search, review of over eighty documents, a review of fire experience and discussions with fire service personnel. This chapter will summarize the findings of the study.

FIRE HAZARD—HARD TO FIND AND DIFFICULT TO EXTINGUISH

The introduction of cellulose insulation into a house or apartment building creates a significant and unique hazard.

The hazard is unique since even properly fire retardant treated cellulose insulation, heated sufficiently, will smolder. Other commonly used construction materials such as solid wood framing, kraft faced fiberglass insulation, and plywood decking are not normally subject to smoldering.

The hazard resulting from the use of newspaper-based cellulose insulation is significant since fire can spread through concealed spaces. The fire may spread undetected by occupants. Accessibility for manual fire fighting is poor. Further, once a smoldering reaction is initiated in the cellulose insulation it is very difficult to stop. To be sure of extinguishment, the cellulose insulation must be removed from the building, separated and submerged or soaked in water.

Adverse fire experience has been identified with cellulose insulation.

SOME EXAMPLES OF FIRE EXPERIENCE

A fire in January 1992 in Havre de Grace, Maryland was started by electrical wiring in the attic of a home. The fire department extinguished the fire and departed. After approximately twenty hours, "a fire of more serious magnitude developed" as the fire rekindled in attic loose-fill cellulose insulation [6]. A somewhat similar fire occurred in Columbia, Maryland, also in January 1992. In this case, the fire started in the kitchen of a dwelling. The fire was extinguished and the fire department left. Approximately four hours later, the fire rekindled in attic cellulose insulation.

An August 31, 1992 kitchen fire occurred in Santa Cruz County, California. In this case, a fire started in the kitchen of a dwelling and exposed cellulose attic insulation. A smoldering reaction was initiated in the cellulose insulation. Three fire department engine companies were "on-scene" for approximately six hours. Eventually, ceilings were pulled down and the cellulose insulation was removed from the building [7].

A number of fires have resulted from cellulose insulation being exposed to chimneys, flue connections, and electrical devices. For example, a January 1986 fire at a Canton, Minnesota cabinet shop is blamed on a chimney from a wood burning stove igniting cellulose attic insulation. The fire completely destroyed the building [8]. Another fire started near a furnace surrounded by cellulose insulation in Sandy, Utah. Fire fighters reportedly spent six hours shoveling cellulose insulation from the attic. The fire department left the premises but were called back four hours later. The second fire was "even larger than before." The second fire "left the house without a roof and nearly gutted." Attic fires caused by cellulose insulation being blown in and around flue pipes led the Flagstaff Fire Department to issue an Alert Bulletin in November 1992.

Another typical fire involving loose-fill cellulose insulation is reported as having started in the concealed attic space of a one story Charles City, Iowa restaurant. The fire caused major damage to the structure [9]. The building was equipped with a drop ceiling, creating a concealed roof-ceiling space. Twelve inches of brown cellulose insulation was used in the concealed space. Investigators believe faulty wiring ignited the shredded paper insulation, and the insulation smoldered for a period of time before the fire was discovered.

Finally, in 1992 during a three-month period, the Philadelphia Housing Development Corporation experienced four fires in attics. The fires occurred within twenty-four hours of the installation of cellulose insulation. The fires were attributed to "tight packed" cellulose insulation and electrical failures [10].

MODEL CODES AND ASTM E84 REQUIREMENTS

The CABO-One and Two Family Dwelling Code (OTFDC), ICBO-Uniform Building Code (UBC), BOCA-National Building Code (NBC), and SBCCI-Standard Building Code (SBC) all impose a "base" requirement for "exposed" insulation and mandate a flame spread rating of twenty-five or less with an accompanying smoke developed factor of 450 or less as determined by ASTM E84 "tunnel test" [11-14]. The OTFDC (1993 revisions), UBC (1994 edition), and SBC (1994 edition) also stipulate that loose fill insulation which cannot be held in the ceiling position of the ASTM E84 "tunnel" without artificial support must be tested on the floor of the tunnel in accordance with the CAN S102.2.

The special requirements for cellulosic attic floor insulation are supplemental to the "base" tunnel limits.

MODEL CODES AND CPSC REQUIREMENTS

The current editions of the BOCA-NBC and SBCCI-SBC require compliance with Consumer Products Safety Commission (CPSC) flammability regulations [13, 14]. The CPSC regulations (16 CFR, Part 1209) require cellulose insulation to be tested in two procedures [15]. One procedure is designed to assess flame spread—the Attic Flooring Radiant Panel Test—whereas a second procedure is designed to evaluate smoldering tendencies.

The Attic Flooring Radiant Panel Test (ASTM E970) determines the minimum radiant heat energy required to be impinged upon the insulation surface to sustain flame propagation. Summer daytime temperatures on the underside of the roof of an attic may reach 160°F [16]. Such temperatures result in radiant heat transfer to the floor of the attic approximating 0.08 watts per square centimeter. Considering the possibility of other heat sources in the attic and the additional energy released during the early stages of a fire, a 50 percent safety factor has been added by the CPSC. Cellulose attic floor insulation is required to resist flame propagation for up to 0.12 watts per square centimeter [17].

The CABO-OTFDC (1993 revisions) also requires attic floor insulation to meet the 0.12 watts per square centimeter criteria, but does so by reference to ASTM E970. The ICBO-UBC contains no reference to the CPSC regulations or to ASTM E970.

It should be noted that the CPSC regulations and ASTM E970 are only applicable to cellulosic insulation mounted on attic floors.

Also according to CPSC regulations, cellulose insulation must resist smoldering when placed in an open top, steel box and exposed to a lighted cigarette.

NO CRITERIA FOR FIRE RETARDANT PERMANENCE OR QUALITY CONTROL

No criteria exist within CPSC regulations or U.S. model codes for evaluating the permanence of fire retardant treatments used with cellulose insulation; nor are there specific criteria for periodic quality control tests to verify product performance either as newly manufactured or as installed.

PROBLEMS WITH NEWLY MANUFACTURED PRODUCT

Newly manufactured loose-fill cellulose insulation sometimes does not meet required firesafety performance [18-22]. In the last report to Congress in 1981, the CPSC reported a 65 percent failure rate—forty-one of sixty-three newly-manufactured cellulose samples failed to meet the CPSC flammability standards [21]. In another study, 175 newly-manufactured cellulose samples were tested by the California Bureau of Home Furnishings and Thermal Insulation (CBHFTI) [22]. Nearly one-fourth of the samples failed flame spread testing. The CBHFTI recently conducted tests on cellulose insulation for the State of Minnesota. A number of newly-manufactured samples failed. In 1992, CBHFTI prohibited two manufacturers from selling cellulose insulation in California because their newly manufactured products failed flammability tests.

SMOLDERING COMBUSTION

Loose-fill cellulose insulation is subject to smoldering. Smoldering provides a means for a product to reach flaming combustion via a heat source too low to directly produce a flame [23]. Smoldering is generally limited to porous materials capable of forming a char. Air is able to diffuse into the smoldering material through the char, supporting a glowing reaction deep within the material. The glowing reaction may not be visible from outside [24]. Once a smoldering reaction is initiated, it may proceed undetected for hours prior to reaching an open flaming stage.

Extinguishment by application of water to the surface of smoldering cellulose insulation may not be effective because water cannot penetrate to the interior. Extinguishment may require removal of the smoldering cellulose insulation from a building and submerging it in water.

Both treated and non-treated loose-fill cellulose insulation will smolder given exposure to temperatures above 450°F [15, 25]. Temperatures above 450°F have been measured in experiments involving "over-lamped" lighting fixtures at the Oak Ridge National Laboratory (ORNL) [26]. Such fixtures have been shown capable of initiating a smoldering reaction, in cellulose insulation which in some cases will proceed to open flames. The research at ORNL resulted in the following conclusions:

> Dangerous operating temperatures were observed when recessed (lighting) fixtures were covered with loose-fill cellulose insulation.

> It has been clearly demonstrated that the misapplication of cellulose (insulation) above recessed light fixtures is a fire hazard.

FLAME PROPAGATION

Traditional combustible materials used in attic floor construction—materials like wood joists or plywood—require 0.12 to 0.18 watts per square centimeter to spread flames across their surface. Therefore, properly treated fire retardant cellulose insulation, in theory, should perform no worse than traditional combustible materials. However, despite the theory there are differences.

Wood framing members in an attic floor assembly achieve their performance through inherent characteristics—no fire retardant additives are used. Therefore, problems associated with applying effective fire retardants are avoided. Furthermore, the solid wood members are not subject to smoldering. Also, significant differences have been observed in the speed with which flame travels across the surface of solid wood members as compared to cellulose loose-fill insulation. For example, in flooring radiant panel tests, flame spread twenty-five times faster over cellulose insulation compared to ordinary (untreated) wood members [27].

Untreated cellulose loose-fill insulation has been shown capable of rapid spread of flame over its surface under attic ambient conditions [16].

FIRE RETARDANT TREATMENTS

Fire retardant chemicals are intended to make ground-up newspaper resistant to smoldering and flame spread. Fire retardants in use today include borax, boric acid, aluminum sulfate, ammonium sulfate, aluminum phosphate, and ammonium phosphate. The fire retardants used to reduce smoldering tendencies (boric acid, for example) are different from those used to reduce surface flame spread (borax, for example). Fire retardant chemicals used to reduce surface flame spread may be antagonistic to the chemicals used to retard smoldering. For example, the sodium in borax, as with all alkali materials, is a catalyst promoting smoldering [28, 29].

THE CORRECT QUANTITY AND MIX
IS REQUIRED

For borates, a fire retardant chemical loading of 20 to 25 percent is required to provide adequate flammability behavior for cellulose insulation. An "optimum formulation" ratio of 5-8:1 boric acid to borax has been reported [22]. Differing ratios may result in poor behavior as excess borax may counteract the smolder inhibiting effects of boric acid. It is very important that *both* the proper mix and minimum 20 to 25 percent loading of fire retardants be maintained over the expected "life" of cellulose insulation.

AGING CHARACTERISTICS OF
CELLULOSE INSULATION

The inability of cellulose to perform adequately after installation has been noted in a number of studies. The City of Palo Alto, California became concerned about the behavior of cellulose insulation in attics. Samples were removed from 133 homes. Of 133 samples tested, only eight passed both CPSC Fire Tests [20].

A ten-year study is underway by the CBHFTI. The results of the study for the first three years are now available [2]. Data indicate there may be a lack of uniformity of chemical loading from bag to bag for the same product. Data also show that boric acid and borax concentration is being reduced. The cause of these effects is undetermined. The results of these effects, as might be expected, are lowered flammability performance. Flame spread performance was significantly affected after only six months of aging. Samples consistently failed flame spread tests after twelve months. After twenty-four months, smoldering tests became "erratic" [4, 5].

In another study, samples of cellulose insulation which had been installed a minimum of two years were removed from twenty-three residential attics located in different areas of the country [3]. Of the twenty-three samples tested for smoldering combustion, fifteen failed—a 65 percent failure rate. Of the nineteen samples tested for flame spread, ten failed—a 53 percent failure rate.

It has become clear that an "aging" problem exists with fire retardant treated cellulose insulation. Satisfactory fire experience with cellulose insulation relies almost exclusively on preventing ignition.

CONCLUSIONS AND SUMMARY

Cellulose insulation consists principally of ground-up newspaper and chemicals. Ground-up newspaper will burn. Chemical additives are used to provide smoldering and flame spread resistance. One chemical is used to add smoldering resistance. A second chemical, used to retard flame spread, may increase smoldering tendencies. Therefore, both the proper mix (ratio) and the correct total chemical load must be maintained for the life of an installation if satisfactory performance is to be achieved.

Newly manufactured cellulose insulation has been tested and failed to meet flammability tests.

"Aging" studies have shown reductions occur in fire retardant "loading" in cellulose insulation over time. An increased tendency for flame spread has been noted in as little as six months. Cellulose insulation installed twelve months or more may lose the ability to retard fire and once ignited may readily spread flame.

Improperly treated cellulose is a fire hazard. Shredded newspaper may readily spread flames under ambient conditions leading to rapid fire involvement of concealed spaces. "Hidden" fires in concealed spaces may develop undetected. Poor access to concealed spaces limits fire fighting effectiveness.

Loose-fill cellulose insulation creates a significantly increased hazard over other commonly used construction materials. It has been shown that both fire retardant treated and non-fire retardant treated cellulose loose-fill insulation exposed to temperatures above 450°F may suffer a propagating, smoldering reaction. Smoldering fires in cellulose insulation are difficult to detect. Extinguishment may require removal of the insulation from the building.

Fires involving cellulose insulation have led to special "alert" bulletins being issued by fire service agencies. Fires have been reported in which cellulose insulation was ignited by inadequate separation from electrical appliances and heat-producing equipment. Other fires have been reported in which the cellulose insulation "rekindles."

The best strategy for good fire protection is to eliminate a hazard. First, quality control measures should be implemented to assure newly manufactured insulation meets flammability standards. Second, if permanent fire retardant treatments cannot be developed, cellulose—shredded newspaper—insulation should be avoided. Products whose intrinsic properties provide adequate performance should be used.

REFERENCES

1. J. R. Lawson, *Environmental Cycling of Cellulosic Thermal Insulation and Its Influence on Fire Performance,* NBSIR 84-2917, Center for Fire Research, National Bureau of Standards, August 1984.
2. S. J. Fischer, R. L. Hillier, and G. Damant, *Long-term Aging Studies on Loose-Fill Cellulose Insulation: Part V,* California Bureau of Home Furnishings and Thermal Insulation, undated.
3. T. Dowds, L. Infante, and E. Pentz, A Field Study of the Fire Resistance Characteristics of Aged Loose-Fill Insulations, *Firesafety and Thermal Insulation, 90,* November 1990.
4. R. L. Hillier and G. H. Damant, *Long-term Aging Studies on Loose-Fill Cellulose Insulation—Part III,* Firesafety and Thermal Insulation Conference, 1990.

5. S. J. Fischer, R. L. Hillier, and G. H. Damant, *Long-term Aging Studies on Loose-Fill Cellulose Insulation: Part IV,* California Bureau of Home Furnishings and Thermal Insulation Interim Report, undated.

6. *Fire Marshals Quarterly,* published by the Fire Marshals Association of North America, Summer 1992.

7. *California Fire Incident Reporting System Incident,* Report Number 92-100747-000.

8. State of Iowa, Department of Public Safety, Field Investigation Report, Case Number 8601073.

9. *Fire Journal,* published by the National Fire Protection Association, Quincy, Massachusetts, March 1985.

10. J. Allegretti, Director, Home Improvement Program, Philadelphia Housing Development Corporation, *Memorandum to All Roofing/Insulation Contractors,* November 11, 1992.

11. *One and Two Family Dwelling Code—1992,* published by the Council of American Building Officials, Paragraphs R-217.2 and R-217.3, 1992.

12. *Uniform Building Code—1991,* published by the International Conference of Building Officials, Paragraph 1714(c), 1991.

13. *National Building Code—1993,* published by Building Officials and Code Administrators International, Inc., Section 722, 1993.

14. *Standard Building Code—1991,* published by the Southern Building Code Congress International, Inc., Section 719, 1991.

15. *Federal Register, 44*:131, Friday, July 6, 1979.

16. D. Gross, *A Preliminary Study of the Firesafety of Thermal Insulation for Use in Attics or Enclosed Spaces in Residential Housing,* NBSIR 78-1497, Center for Fire Research, National Bureau of Standards, July 1978.

17. S. Davis, *Technical Rationale for the General Services Administration Federal Specification HH-I-515D, Flame Resistance Provisions,* Center for Fire Research, National Bureau of Standards, December 1978.

18. Owens Corning Fiberglas Technical Bulletin, *Two Year Insulation Materials Study,* March 1980.

19. State of California, Department of Consumer Affairs, Bureau of Home Furnishings and Thermal Insulation, Report No. 160-91 (November 27, 1991), Report No. 155-91 (November 26, 1991), Report No. 169-91 (January 2, 1992), and Report No. 19-92 (March 26, 1992).

20. D. Katz and S. A. Siddiqui, *Cellulose Insulation Issue in Palo Alto—History and Current Status,* proceedings of Second California Thermal Insulation International Conference, 1989.

21. CPSC Report to Congress, *Report of Enforcement Activities, Interim Safety Standards for Cellulose Insulation,* August 24, 1981.

22. S. A. Siddiqui, R. L. Hillier, and G. H. Damant, *Effect of Fire Retardant Formulations on the Fire Properties of Cellulose Insulation,* Fall Conference of the Fire Retardant Chemicals Association, October 1987.

23. *SFPE Handbook of Fire Protection Engineering,* (1st Edition), published by the Society of Fire Protection Engineers, Boston, Massachusetts, Section 1/Chapter 23, 1988.

24. *Fire Protection Handbook,* (17th Edition), published by the National Fire Protection Association, Quincy, Massachusetts, Section 1/Chapter 6 and Section 3/Chapter 2, 1991.

25. W. A. Kleinfelder, *Investigation of the Fire Performance of Building Insulation in Full Scale and Laboratory Fire Tests,* prepared by Underwriters Laboratories, under Subcontract No. 7863 for Oak Ridge National Laboratory, April 1984.
26. D. W. Yarbrough, K. T. Yoo, and P. B. Koneru, *Recessed Light Fixture Test Facility,* contract no. W-7405-eng-26, Oak Ridge National Laboratory, Oak Ridge, Tennessee, July 1979.
27. *ASTM E970 Radiant Panel Test Results for Wood Components found in Attics,* report no. 50091, Owens Corning Fiberglas Technical Center, January 13, 1992.
28. L. A. Issen, *Fire Performance of Loose-Fill Cellulosic Insulation in Residential Occupancies—A Progress Report,* NBSIR 80-2085, Center for Fire Research, National Bureau of Standards, August 1980.
29. M. J. Williams, *Cellulose Fiber Insulation—The Effect of Chemical Formulation on Fire Test Properties,* Fire Retardant Chemicals Association Meeting, March 1980.

CHAPTER 8

Regulating Foam Plastic Insulated Garage Doors: A Summary of Research for the National Association of Garage Door Manufacturers

Donald W. Belles

Foam plastic insulated garage doors are subject to specific regulation in the Uniform Building Code (UBC). Product flammability performance is evaluated in UBC Standard 26-3—a room/corner test. UBC Standard 26-3 pass/fail criteria are subjective and product acceptability is based upon visual observations.

An updated room/corner test has been developed for assessing the flammability behavior of foam plastic insulated garage doors. The updated test procedure uses a diffusion burner as the fire source. Measurements of heat release and smoke release are used to judge product acceptance. Heat release and smoke release limits have been related to hazard using hand calculations and computer models.

Products using foam plastic insulation are regulated by the 1994 edition of the Uniform Building Code (UBC), Volume 1, Chapter 26.

UBC 2602.5.4 regulates "doors" using foam plastic insulation. 2602.5.4 was written to regulate foam plastic insulated pedestrian doors in building applications where a fire resistive rating is not required.

Existing UBC Paragraph 2602.5.4 is prescriptive. Foam plastic insulation having a flame spread rating of seventy-five or less (and presumably a smoke developed value of 450 or less) is allowed in doors. The door facing, must provide a substantial ignition barrier consisting of a minimum 0.016 in. steel or 0.032 in. aluminum. The normal thermal barrier requirement is "waived" for doors meeting these prescriptive requirements.

A review of existing 2602.5.4 raises numerous questions:

1. Although 2602.5.4 was written to deal with pedestrian doors, are the provisions applicable to foam plastic insulated garage doors?
2. Assuming 2602.5.4 is applicable to garage doors and considering the setting (automobiles, fuels, combustible storage, and the like) in which garage doors are used, are the requirements reasonable?
3. Assuming the requirements of 2602.5.4 are applicable to garage doors, what level of fire safety is required and how would one determine compliance?
4. Since the provisions of 2602.5.4 are prescriptive, what level of performance is required for code compliance for those doors which have nonmetallic facings or thinner metal facings than now allowed?

This chapter will attempt to respond to these questions. Information will also be included on room corner fire tests of foam plastic insulated garage doors conducted at Omega Point Laboratories by the National Association of Garage Door Manufacturers (NAGDM). The author served as consultant to NAGDM for the fire testing program.

EXISTING REGULATION OF GARAGE DOORS

The ICBO staff have interpreted UBC 2602.5.4 to apply to foam plastic insulated garage doors. Paragraph 2602.5.4 mandates metallic facings having a specified minimum thickness. Doors having nonmetallic facings or metal facings less than the thickness specified would require specific approval based on "approved tests" in accordance with UBC 2602.6. The approved tests are to evaluate products in a fashion "related to actual end use." Historically, UBC Standard 26-3 (formerly UBC Standard 17-5) has been used as the test method for conducting such evaluations.

UBC Standard 26-3 is a room corner test using a 30 lb. wood crib as the ignition source. Products undergoing evaluation are typically mounted as full assemblies over two 8 ft. by 8 ft. areas on two walls joined at a right angle to form a corner (see Figure 1). The crib is placed in the corner adjacent to the products being tested and is ignited. The crib burns for fifteen minutes. To perform satisfactorily, a product must resist propagating flames to the extremity of the test specimen. It is sometimes difficult to visually judge whether or not flames reach the end of an 8 ft. wide specimen. Char depths (for thermoset products) exceeding 1/4 in. are considered evidence of flaming. The performance of thermoplastics (which melt) is not treated, and such behavior is subject to interpretation and judgment.

Smoke levels generated during UBC 26-3 testing are restricted. UBC 26-3 states "smoke levels generated during the test period shall not be excessive." A product's "smoke performance" is judged visually using videotapes of experiments. The visual appearance of smoke exiting the fire room door will vary,

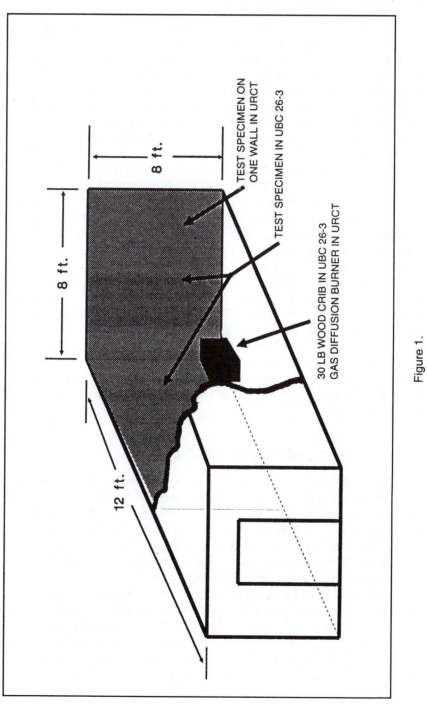

TEST SPECIMEN ON ONE WALL IN URCT

TEST SPECIMEN IN UBC 26-3

30 LB WOOD CRIB IN UBC 26-3
GAS DIFFUSION BURNER IN URCT

8 ft.

8 ft.

12 ft.

Figure 1.

depending upon lighting conditions and the quality and position of the camera. Conditions of acceptance for smoke are subjective.

Garage door manufacturers have been directed to test their products in accordance with UBC 26-3 because UBC 2602.5.4 has been interpreted to be applicable. In accordance with UBC 26-3, manufacturers have been required to install two garage doors joined at right angles to form a corner for testing. Such a test arrangement does not reflect actual installations as garage doors would seldom, if ever, be installed to form a corner in a building. Such a test arrangement is contrary to the intent of 2602.6, as 2602.6 stipulates products are to be mounted as intended for use. Furthermore, UBC Standard 26-3 is listed in UBC 2602.6 as a type of test that *could* be used. UBC 2602.6 indicates specific approval can be obtained by conducting "fire tests related to actual end use *such as* UBC Standard 26-3." UBC 2602.6 allows other types of tests providing the product is mounted as intended for use and assuming the ignition source is representative of those likely to be experienced during product use.

UBC Standard 26-3 was developed in the 60s and adopted by the UBC in the mid-70s. The method represented the best available technology at the time it was developed. Perhaps the time has come to update the procedure. The subjective pass/fail criteria of the current UBC Standard 26-3 leaves the manufacturer and the building official uncertain as to product acceptability. An improved version of the room corner test procedure is available. Instrumentation and measurements can be substituted for subjective visual observations of performance. An improved room/corner test procedure was used to characterize the flammability behavior of a variety of foam plastic insulated garage doors in this research project.

UPDATED ROOM/CORNER TEST

The Updated Room Corner Test (URCT) method utilized for this project is similar to existing UBC Standard 8-2 (formerly UBC Standard 42-2). The big difference between UBC 26-3 and the URCT is the use of a gas diffusion burner and a hood/duct exhaust system for collecting smoke. Analysis of the smoke through instruments in the hood/duct exhaust system allow calculation of rate of heat release via oxygen consumption. Smoke release rates are determined by an optical system for measurement of light obscuration.

In the URCT, use of a diffusion burner (with known heat output) allows calculation of a product's net rate of heart disease. Rate of heat release is perhaps the single most important parameter of product performance that determines hazard. Rate of heat release can be related to temperature rise in a room. Equally important, rate of heat release is proportional to mass consumed during a fire, as in:

$$q = m*H_c$$

Where:

q = rate of heat release (kW)
m = mass lost rate (kg/s)
H_c = heat of combustion (kJ/kg)

Therefore, rate of heat release is proportional to mass concentrations in a smoke layer. If the mass concentration of smoke is known, vision distance can be estimated. The "toxic quality" of the smoke is also related to the mass concentration of gases. "Dose" is determined by concentration and time of exposure. In simple terms, if a product produces low heat release rates, the product is unlikely to represent a hazard from either heat or smoke. Conversely, products that evolve high heat release rates will generally represent a hazard from both heat and smoke.

In the URCT, smoke is collected in an exhaust hood/duct system. The percent light transmission (%T) is determined over a path length (l) during an exhaust flow (V/s). Optical density (OD) is calculated as log (100/%T). Multiplying OD/l times V/s produces a smoke release rate [SRR (m²s)]. Vision distance can be estimated by integrating the smoke release rate over time as follows [1]:

$$\int_0^t SRR\ (dt) * \left(\frac{1}{\text{Roman Volume Selected}} \right) = \frac{OD}{l} m^{-1} \text{ (For Room Volume Selected)}$$

OD/l and extinction coefficient (K) are related as:

$$K = 2.3*(OD/l)m^{-1}$$

Vision distance (S) is related to extinction coefficient for light emitting signs by:

$$K * S = 8$$

Where:

K = extinction coefficient (m^{-1})
S = vision distance (m)

Accordingly, vision distance to rear illuminated exit signs can be estimated for smoke produced by a product during the URCT when the smoke is distributed in a given volume.

A thermocouple placed in the foam plastic core of the test specimen is used in the URCT to determine if flames reach the extremity of a test specimen. Thermocouples are also provided in the fire room to record upper layer temperatures. A calorimeter, located near floor level and facing up, records total heat flux.

The effect of the fire on objects in or near the room, but remote from the ignition source, is evaluated mainly by measurements of total heat flux incident on the floor, upper layer gas temperatures and the peak rate of heat release. The effect of the fire on areas remote from the room of origin is evaluated mainly by the measurement of total heat release.

The ignition source in the URCT is the same as that prescribed in the UBC Standard 8-2. The burner output is 40 kW for five minutes, followed by 150 kW for ten minutes. A 40 kW exposure involves a $2^1/_2$-3 ft. high flame that represents a waste basket sized fire. The exposure determines if the flames from a localized fire will spread over the surface of a garage door to objects remote from the fire origin. After a five minute, 40 kW exposure, the burner output is increased to 150 kW for an additional ten minutes. A 150 kW flame will reach to the 8 ft. ceiling of the fire room without any contribution by the product being tested. The 150 kW exposure is based upon the presumption that the initial waste basket sized fire ignites a second, larger object. The 150 kW exposure determines if the garage door is likely to produce sufficient amounts of heat to create a hazard or to cause full room involvement or flashover. The fire exposure conditions selected (40 kW/150 kW) are sufficient to cause flashover for a room lined with fire retardant treated wood paneling. Ordinary wood paneling, exposed to the same conditions, will produce flames reaching to the room door between 6 and 7 minutes and will lead to flashover at about eight to nine minutes.

Finally, in the URCT, foam plastic insulated garage doors are mounted on one wall in the fire room. An 8 ft. wide by 7 ft. high garage door assembly is mounted on the 8 ft. by 8 ft. wall opposite the wall with the doorway. Specimen mounting simulates actual installation practices (Figure 1).

PRODUCT CHARACTERISTICS IN TODAY'S MARKET

A variety of garage door constructions have been tested in the URCT as follows:

1. Product A—Steel pan, laminated expanded polystyrene insulation (7/8 in. thick) with Kraft-polyethylene facer.
2. Product B—Steel pan, loose expanded polystyrene ($1^1/_2$ in. thick with polystyrene facer).
3. Product C—Wood sandwich with expanded polystyrene ($1^1/_4$ in. thick) with $^1/_8$ in. wood face veneer.
4. Product D—Steel sandwich using expanded polystyrene (2 in. thick) and a 0.012 in. steel facing.
5. Product E—Wood panel, no insulation.
6. Product F—Steel pan, polyurethane foam ($^5/_8$ in. thick) with foil-Kraft facing.
7. Product G—Steel pan, polyurethane foam ($1^3/_8$ in. thick), 0.010 in. steel facing.
8. Product GG—Replicate test of Product G.

9. Product H—Steel pan, loose expanded polystyrene insulation ($1^1/_2$ in. thick) with Kraft-polyethylene facing.
10. Product HH—Replicate test of Product H.

The eight garage door assemblies tested are representative of a majority of products using foam plastic insulation in today's market. Testing a representative sampling of actual products provides a "feel" for how existing products would perform in the URCT. This data allows a determination of hazard with respect to existing products and assesses the impact of the URCT on the current market.

As might be expected, product performance varies, depending upon construction details. Of the eight products tested, two were judged to perform unsatisfactorily. Products having 0.010 in. steel and $^1/_8$ in. wood facings were judged to perform adequately.

Net rate of heat release (kW) for the eight garage door specimens is illustrated on Figure 2. Smoke release rate (m^2/s) and total smoke release (m^2) are illustrated on Figures 3 and 4, respectively. Upper layer fire room temperatures are shown on Figure 5. A data summary for the eight products tested is contained in Figure 6.

PRODUCT PERFORMANCE V. HAZARD

A revision to UBC 2602 has been developed which proposes to reference the URCT. Pass/fail criteria have been developed for foam plastic insulated garage doors. The pass/fail criteria have been developed based on hazard analysis using hand calculations and computer fire models.

Rate of heat release measurements can be related to room temperatures via hand calculations [2] or computer models [3]. For example, Figure 7 compares upper layer temperatures from URCT garage door tests to computer fire model predictions. It will be noted there is good agreement between the computer generated predictions and actual measurements.

A heat release limit must be selected to control hazards and set performance levels for garage doors using foam plastic insulation. One can look to results of hazard assessments and existing code precedents for a suggested limit. For example, UBC Standard 8-2 sets a 300 kW limit for textile wall coverings. NFPA 101, Life Safety Code, sets a 250 kW limit for furnishings in correctional and detention facilities. The Uniform Fire Code, Article II, has a 100 kW limit for exhibit booth construction and stage sets, whereas decorative objects are limited to 150 kW.

A computer analysis has been performed [4]. The analysis assumes a 250 kW fire in a two car garage. An open doorway leads from the garage to the living area of a dwelling. Fire duration is based on the time required for a 250 kW fire to consume the combustible content of a typical foam plastic insulated garage door (see Figures 8-10). The model predicts the smoke layer drops to floor level in the garage and interconnected living-dining area in around 400 seconds. Garage

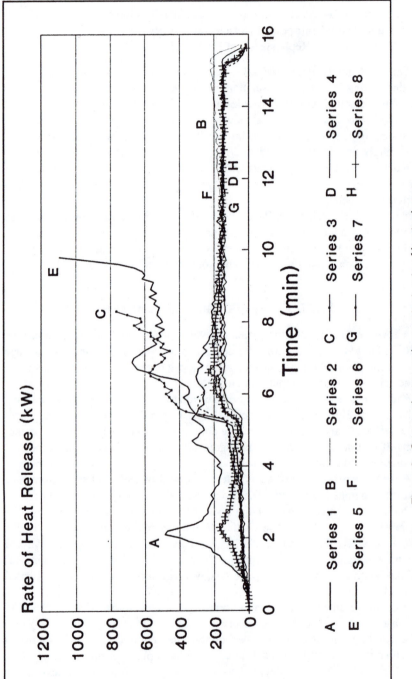

Figure 2. Garage door room/corner test, rate of heat release.

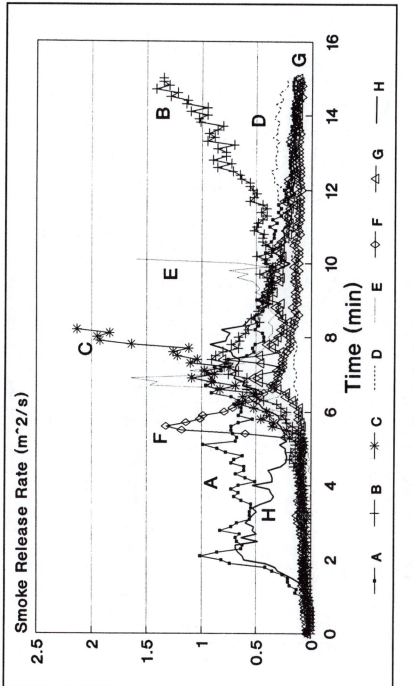

Figure 3. Smoke release rate.

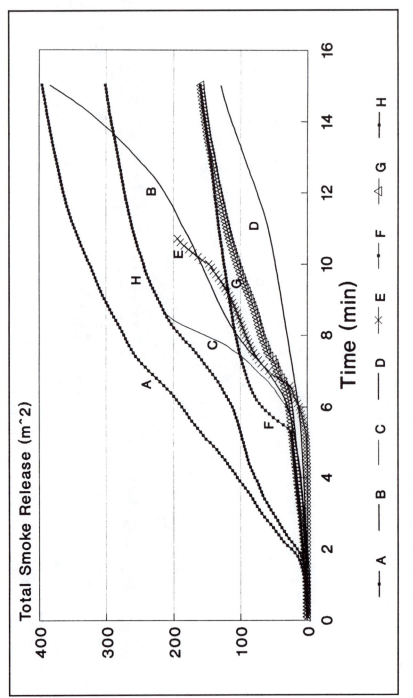

Figure 4. Total heat release.

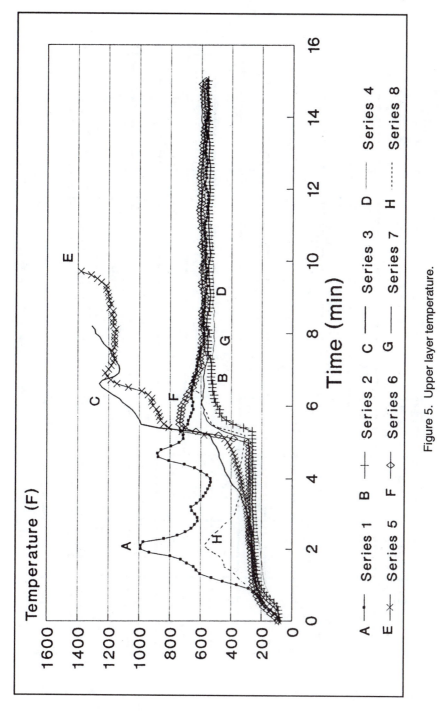

Figure 5. Upper layer temperature.

PRODUCT	MAX RHR (kW)[3]	MAX[4] SRR (M^2/S)	TSR[4] 5 MIN (M^2)	TSR[4] 7.5 MIN (M^2)	MAX CORE TEMP (C)	THR [2] (MJ)	MAX TEMP UPPER LAYER (C)
A	447	1.01	145	260	609	175	532
B	60	1.42	18	84	197	112	297
C	615[1]	2.13[1]	16	106[1]	651 [1]	[1]	710 [1]
D	6	0.38	9	26	254	91.1	304
E	947[1]	1.60[1]	1	80 [1]	733 [1]	[1]	748 [1]
F	149	1.33	22	101	277	112.4	392
G	28	0.81	21	58	232	101.2	319
H	130	0.92	95	166	296	120.1	358
GG	48	0.49	22	68	250	104	324
HH	607	2.77	83	174	586	174	617

(1) TEST TERMINATED PRIOR TO 15 MINUTES
(2) INCLUDES BURNER OUTPUT
(3) PRODUCT ONLY

(4) CALCULATED PER ASTM E1537 USING OPTICAL DENSITY (LOG 100/%T)

Figure 6. Data summary — URCT.

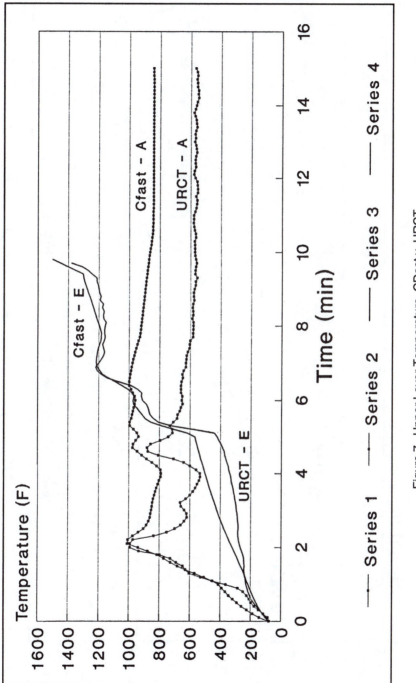

Figure 7. Upper Layer Temperature, CDast v. URCT.

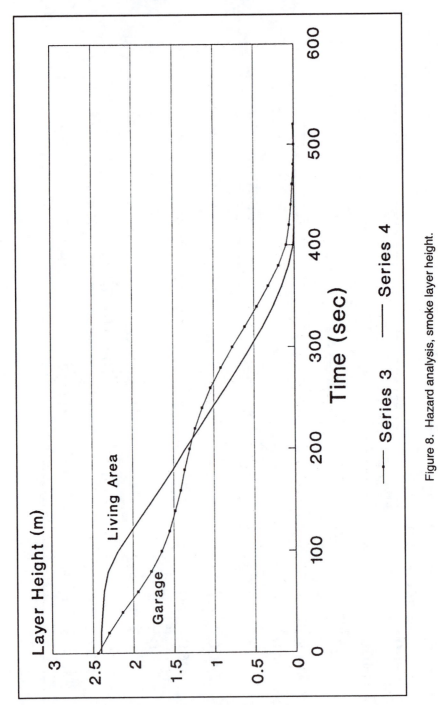

Figure 8. Hazard analysis, smoke layer height.

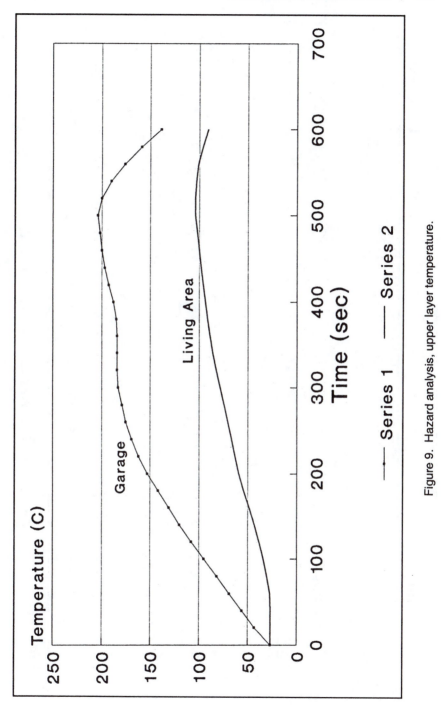

Figure 9. Hazard analysis, upper layer temperature.

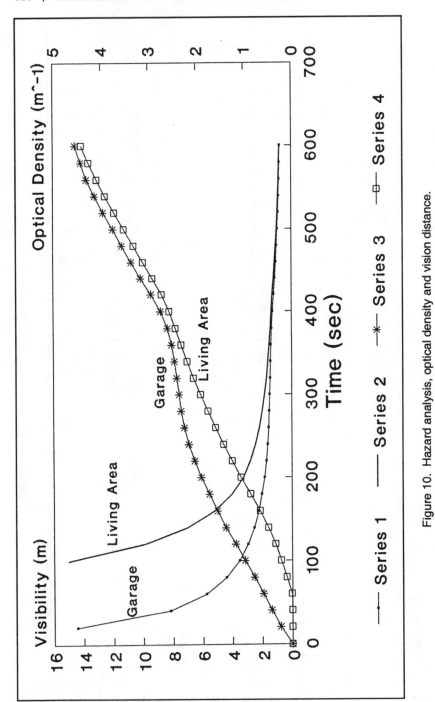

Figure 10. Hazard analysis, optical density and vision distance.

temperatures at 400 seconds approach 200°C, whereas temperatures in the living area are predicted to peak around 100°C at about 500 seconds. The analysis indicates a garage door that releases a maximum of 250 kW will create hazardous conditions in a two car garage in about 150 to 200 seconds, assuming no smoke vents to the outside from the garage. The living spaces of the dwelling should be tenable for an extended period of time. A 250 kW heat release limit will adequately limit the contribution of foam plastic insulated garage doors to hazard and provides reasonable acceptance criteria for the burning behavior of such doors.

The effect of smoke on vision distance can be assessed in different ways. Figures 11 and 12 illustrate the impact of smoke from URCT tests on vision distance assuming the smoke from the test is distributed in a two car garage. It will be noted that products producing higher rates of heat release (therefore consuming greater mass) tend to produce more smoke, limiting vision distance. Product H's effect on vision distance may at first seem contradictory, since Product H's rate of heat release levels are only moderate. The behavior of Product H warrants additional discussion.

Product H illustrates the difference between smoke yield and smoke production. Smoke yield, which is identified in these tests as the smoke release rate, describes the appearance of the smoke at an instant in time. The total production of smoke is more significant for, as smoke accumulates in a given volume, the ability to see through the smoke is affected. Product H shows that a product does not have to have a high smoke yield to produce sufficient smoke to affect vision. Total smoke production is related to the total mass lost by a product as it burns. Consequently, a product that has little mass (but high yield, that is, high smoke release rate) may appear to perform poorly based on short term visual observations during tests. However, if the mass consumed is limited, the effect on vision distance may be insignificant. On the other hand, a product that has a modest yield over an extended time interval may not appear to be a problem, but the total smoke produced may have a significant impact on vision. Product H is an example of a product that has a moderate smoke yield extending over a sufficient period of time to have a significant impact on vision distance. Smoke acceptance criterion in UBC Standard 26-3 is based on visual observations using videotapes. Product acceptability in UBC 26-3 is based on "yield" and does not take total smoke production into account.

It is proposed to limit smoke release during an URCT to that which will allow a light-emitting sign to be visible at 5 meters, five minutes after the start of a test, assuming the smoke from the fire room is distributed in a two car garage. Similarly, it is proposed to limit the smoke release to that which would allow a light-emitting sign to be visible at 2 meters, 7.5 minutes after the start of the test.

Computer modeling was also used to estimate the effect of smoke on vision distance [4]. Figure 10 predicts vision distance to a light emitting exit sign in a two

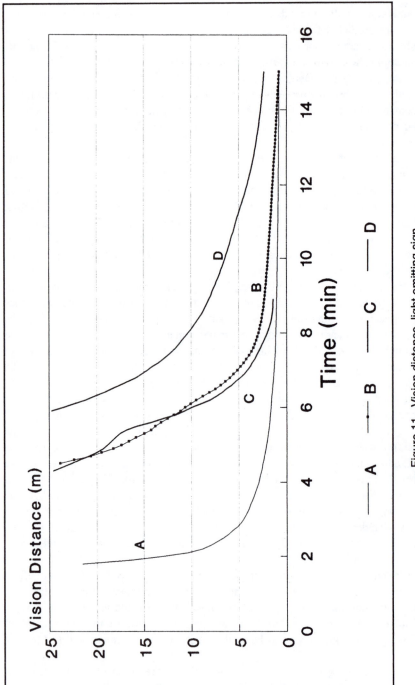

Figure 11. Vision distance, light emitting sign.

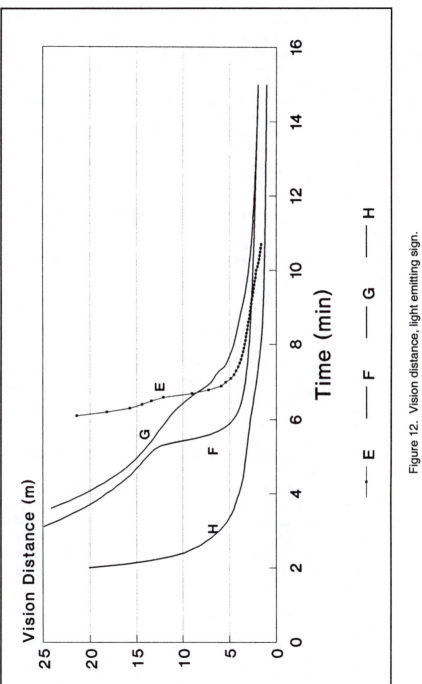

Figure 12. Vision distance, light emitting sign.

car garage and an adjacent living room-dining room space. The analysis is based on a 250 kW fire and assumes a door between the garage and a dwelling living area is open. A light-emitting sign would be visible at approximately 2 meters in the two car garage after about 200 seconds. In the living area, an exit sign would be visible from about 2 meters at 300 seconds. After 600 seconds, a light-emitting sign is predicted to be visible at a maximum of 1 meter in both the garage and living space. Smoke production limits are included in the URCT. A total smoke release of 60 m^2 or less at five minutes and total smoke release 150 m^2 or less at 7.5 minutes are suggested. These limits establish reasonable levels of performance by providing sizable time intervals before vision is reduced.

A temperature rise limit of 750°F is suggested for the combustible core of the garage door. The temperature rise limit is to restrict flame spread to less than the width of the door. As a consequence, one may test an 8 ft. wide door and have confidence the results will apply to doors of greater width. The temperature rise limit will reduce the probability of a product spreading flame to ignite other objects.

SUMMARY

An updated room/corner fire test procedure has been developed for assessing the flammability behavior of foam plastic insulated garage doors. The test procedure uses a diffusion burner as the fire source. Measurements of heat release, smoke release, upper layer temperatures, sample core temperature, and heat flux, are taken to describe product behavior.

Measurements allow setting pass/fail criteria using instrumentation. The measured pass/fail criteria avoids the subjective visual observations required in the existing room/corner test procedure—UBC Standard 26-3.

Acceptance criteria have been developed for foam plastic insulated garage doors. Existing code text for rate of heat release limits have been reviewed, and computer models and hand calculations have been used to develop pass/fail criteria. The pass/fail criteria have been analyzed in terms of product flammability performance. The proposed acceptance criteria will limit the contribution of foam plastic insulated garage doors to fire hazard.

Pass/fail criteria have been suggested as follows:

Maximum net peak rate of heat release—250 kW
Smoke limits:
    Maximum total smoke release of –60 m^2 at 5 minutes
    Maximum total smoke release—150 m^2 at 7.5 minutes
Specimen core temperatures rise remote from the burner—750°F or less.

REFERENCES

1. G. W. Mulholland, *Smoke Production and Properties*, Section 1/Chapter 25, SFPE Handbook of Fire Protection Engineering, First Edition, National Fire Protection Association, 1988.
2. Budnick et al., *Simplified Calculations for Enclosure Fires*, Section 10/Chapter 11, Fire Protection Handbook—Seventeenth Edition, National Fire Protection Association, 1991.
3. R. D. Peacock et al., *CFAST, the Consolidated Model of Fire Growth and Smoke Transport*, NIST Technical Note 1299, National Institute of Standards and Technology, February 1993.
4. W. W. Jones and R. D. Peacock, *Technical Reference Guide for FAST, Version 18*, National Institute of Standards and Technology, Technical Note 1262, May 1989.

CHAPTER 9

Heat Isolation Scenario for a Double Fire Shutter System

R. K. K. Yuen, S. M. Lo, and G. H. Yeoh

In some situations, fire codes may stipulate the use of lobbies to protect openings in compartment walls. However, the use of lobbies will in some cases impair the communication between different parts in a building. The purpose of this chapter is to demonstrate that a double fire shutter system can be an appropriate alternative means of protection to the openings against the spread of flame and heat instead of using lobby enclosures. The effectiveness of the double shutter system will depend on the separation between the shutters and the emissivity of the shutters. A Computational Fluid Dynamics (CFD) technique is used to analyze the influences of the two parameters.

It is recognized that openings at compartment walls will defeat the fire resisting properties of the walls. However, in order to maintain good communication between different spaces in a building, provision of openings at compartment walls becomes necessary. However, such openings should be effectively protected in terms of fire safety.

In Hong Kong, the fire resisting requirements of elements in buildings are governed by the Code of Practice on Fire Resisting Construction, 1996 (FRC Code, 1996) [1]. In accordance with the guidance stipulated in paragraph 10.1 of this Code, openings in compartment walls for communication of adjoining compartments should be protected by a lobby with fire resisting doors.

Hong Kong is a densely populated city and the land supply is scarce. Multi-story high-rise buildings are, therefore, constructed everywhere to satisfy the demand for various uses. Manufacturing plants are also accommodated in multi-story factory buildings along with residential occupancies. These multi-story factory buildings are termed "flatted factory buildings." Raw materials, production parts, and other goods are loaded or unloaded at spaces situated on the ground floor of the building. These items are then conveyed to the factories on upper floors by elevators. The loading and unloading spaces and the landing areas of the elevators must be considered as different compartments and should be separated by walls with adequate fire resistance. Openings protected by lobbies should, therefore, be provided for the communication purpose. However, lobbies will obstruct the smoothness of the conveyance of the materials and goods.

It is found that when buildings are in use, fire rated doors of such lobbies, if provided, will be wedged open by users in order to facilitate the conveyance of materials and goods. In these circumstances, the function of the lobbies will be impaired and in turn the safety level of the building in case of fire will be jeopardized.

The objective of this article is to illustrate an arrangement by which the conveyance of materials and goods through openings in the compartment walls will not be obstructed and the safety level will still be maintained. The proposed alternative approach is to use a double fire shutter system in place of the lobby configuration. This article will also indicate that the effectiveness of the proposed system will be governed by the separation and emissivity of the shutters.

PERFORMANCE REQUIREMENTS

Openings in compartment walls should be protected so that passage of flame and smoke are resisted to an acceptable standard. A protected lobby is considered to have adequate protection if:

1. it resists the spread of flame by doors with adequate fire resistance in terms of integrity, and
2. it resists the spread of flame and smoke by offering a buffer zone (reservoir) for smoke and radiant heat transmission.

Therefore, an alternative means of protection should also have similar resistance to spread of flame and smoke.

The alternative approach by a double fire shutter system is designed so that shutters have a Fire Resistance Period (FRP) equivalent to that of the compartment walls in terms of integrity. The arrangement is shown in Figure 1. The shutters operate upon actuation of smoke detectors installed immediately adjacent to the openings.

If the fire shutters function properly, the resistance of spread of flame can be regarded as adequate as the fire shutters are provided with equal FRP as to the compartment walls in terms of integrity. The question then is whether the fire shutters can also effectively retard the smoke spread and radiant heat transmission.

Control of the operation of the shutters is carried out by smoke detectors installed adjacent to the openings. This indicates that the shutters will be closed once significant amounts of smoke have been detected. Once the shutters have

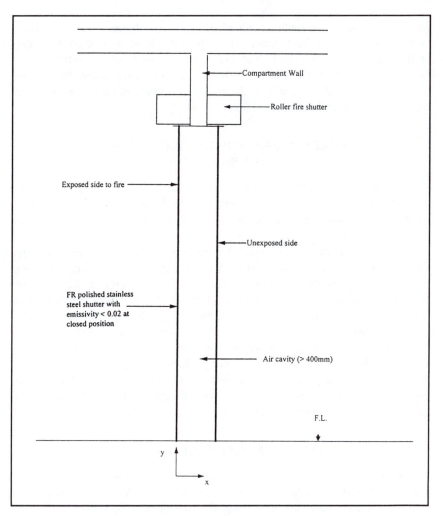

Figure 1. Schematic diagram of the double fire shutter assembly.

closed, the effectiveness of smoke sealing capabilities will depend on the width of the gaps between the shutters and around the flame opening. In practice, if a leakage rate not exceeding $3m^3/m/hour$ when tested at 25 Pa of pressure under BS476 is maintained [2], the smoke checking property of the shutters can be considered as acceptable.

If the arrangement and performance of the shutters can be made as described, the system can effectively resist the spread of fire in terms of integrity and smoke. The remaining question then is whether such system can effectively resist radiant heat transmission. Fire shutters with adequate fire resistance in terms of insulation can resist radiant heat transmission. However, in Hong Kong fire shutters (roller shutter) with adequate insulation property are not available on the market.

The following sections will discuss the possibility of using double fire shutters which are commonly available in the market (i.e., without fire insulation property) to resist radiant heat transmission.

HEAT CONVEYANCE THROUGH DOUBLE FIRE SHUTTERS

The double fire shutter assembly consists basically of two panes of fire shutters. This arrangement can effectively be considered as an insulated assembly to prevent excessive rise of temperature due to heat penetration from the fire side to the unexposed side.

To evaluate the temperature rise at the unexposed side of the arrangement due to conduction, convection, and radiation through the air-cavity formed between the two fire shutters, the computational fluid dynamics (CFD) technique has been employed. This involves the setting up of the essential conservation equations (i.e., Navier-Stokes equations) for mass, momentum, and energy. The radiative transfer is handled by modified discrete ordinates method with participating gas absorption. The equations are solved with appropriate boundary and initial conditions using the FIRE3D computer software package developed jointly by CSIRO, Australia and the Department of Building and Construction, City University of Hong Kong and based on the Finite Volume Technique. The mathematical formulation and computational results are discussed in the next section.

MATHEMATICAL FORMULATION

The mathematical model for the flame spread consists of the three-dimensional, Favre-averaged equations of transport for mass, momentum, and enthalpy. Turbulence is modeled using the two-equation $\kappa-\varepsilon$ model, with the turbulent viscosity given by $\mu_t = c_\mu \rho \kappa^2/\varepsilon$ where ρ is the gas density. The effective viscosity μ_{eff} is obtained as the sum of the molecular and turbulent viscosities. In the κ and ε equations, production of turbulence due to buoyancy and the effect of thermal stratification of the turbulence dissipation rate are included in the G terms. The conservation equations in general form are expressed as:

$$\frac{\partial(\rho\phi)}{\partial t} + \nabla \cdot (\rho \bar{u} \phi) = \nabla \cdot (\Gamma_\phi \nabla \phi) + S_\phi \tag{1}$$

where ϕ represents the field variables; u, v, and w are the velocities; κ and ε are the kinetic energy and dissipation of turbulence; and h is the enthalpy—listed in Table 1); and Γ_ϕ and S_ϕ denote the diffusion coefficient and the source term respectively.

In Table 1, the production rate of turbulent energy P for the turbulent quantities κ and ε is given by

$$P = \mu_t \left\{ 2\left[\left(\frac{\partial u}{\partial x}\right)^2 + \left(\frac{\partial v}{\partial y}\right)^2 + \left(\frac{\partial w}{\partial z}\right)^2\right] + \left(\frac{\partial u}{\partial y} + \frac{\partial v}{\partial x}\right)^2 + \left(\frac{\partial v}{\partial z} + \frac{\partial w}{\partial y}\right)^2 + \left(\frac{\partial u}{\partial z} + \frac{\partial w}{\partial x}\right)^2 \right\} -$$

$$\frac{2}{3}\left[\rho\kappa + \mu_t\left(\frac{\partial u}{\partial x} + \frac{\partial v}{\partial y} + \frac{\partial w}{\partial z}\right)\right]\left(\frac{\partial u}{\partial x} + \frac{\partial v}{\partial y} + \frac{\partial w}{\partial z}\right) \tag{2}$$

while the production of turbulence due to buoyancy G is modeled according to

$$G = g\frac{\mu_t}{\sigma_h}\frac{1}{\rho}\frac{\partial\rho}{\partial y} \tag{3}$$

The closure constants for the κ–ε model are: $c_\mu = 0.09$, $c_1 = 1.44$, $c_2 = 1.92$, $c_3 = 1.44$, $\sigma_\kappa = 1.0$, and $\sigma_\varepsilon = 1.3$. The Prandtl number is $\sigma_h = 0.7$.

Radiation is an essential part of the mathematical model for the problem concerned because of the presence of the combustion products which greatly augment the radiation heat transfer. An efficient and accurate method of radiative transfer—the discrete ordinates method—is employed in the present study. The radiative transfer equation, ignoring any scattering effects in the radiative heat transfer, can be written as follows:

$$\xi_j\frac{\partial I_j}{\partial x} + \eta_j\frac{\partial I_j}{\partial y} + \zeta_j\frac{\partial I_j}{\partial z} = -k_a I_j + k_a E_b \tag{4}$$

where $E_b = \sigma T^4$, σ is the Stefan-Blotzman constant. The direction cosines ξ_j, η_j, and ζ_j represent a set of directions for each of the radiation intensities I_j which span over the total solid angle range of 4π around a point in space; and the integrals over solid angles are approximated using a numerical quadrature. From [3] the S_4 quadrature is employed in the current implementation of the radiation model. The finite volume method is employed to discretize equation (4) and to ensure positive intensities throughout the solution domain, the positive scheme of [4] is applied. The radiation source term S_{rad} is appended to the enthalpy equation (see Table 1) through the expression:

$$S_{rad} = k_a\sum_{j=1}^{N} a_j I_{p,j} - 4k_a\,\sigma T^4 \tag{5}$$

where $N = 24$ for the S_4 quadrature; a_j constitutes the total number of discrete directions of the intensity around a point in a control volume; and the subscript p denotes the central grid point of the control volume. k_a is the gas absorption coefficient and is taken to be $0.1\ m^{-1}$ which corresponds in general to the value of the combustion products (i.e., CO_2 and H_2O).

Table 1. Transport Equations for Variable ϕ in the Flow Field

ϕ	Γ_ϕ	S_ϕ
1	0	0
u	μ_{eff}	$-\dfrac{\partial}{\partial x}\left[p+\dfrac{2}{3}\bar{\rho}\kappa+\dfrac{2}{3}(\mu_{eff})\left(\dfrac{\partial u}{\partial x}+\dfrac{\partial v}{\partial y}+\dfrac{\partial w}{\partial z}\right)\right]+\dfrac{\partial}{\partial x}\left((\mu_{eff})\dfrac{\partial u}{\partial x}\right)$ $+\dfrac{\partial}{\partial y}\left((\mu_{eff})\dfrac{\partial v}{\partial x}\right)+\dfrac{\partial}{\partial z}\left((\mu_{eff})\dfrac{\partial w}{\partial x}\right)$
v	μ_{eff}	$-\dfrac{\partial}{\partial y}\left[p+\dfrac{2}{3}\bar{\rho}\kappa+\dfrac{2}{3}(\mu_{eff})\left(\dfrac{\partial u}{\partial x}+\dfrac{\partial v}{\partial y}+\dfrac{\partial w}{\partial z}\right)\right]+\dfrac{\partial}{\partial x}\left((\mu_{eff})\dfrac{\partial u}{\partial y}\right)$ $+\dfrac{\partial}{\partial y}\left((\mu_{eff})\dfrac{\partial v}{\partial y}\right)+\dfrac{\partial}{\partial z}\left((\mu_{eff})\dfrac{\partial w}{\partial y}\right)-(\rho-\rho_0)g$
w	μ_{eff}	$-\dfrac{\partial}{\partial z}\left[p+\dfrac{2}{3}\bar{\rho}\kappa+\dfrac{2}{3}(\mu_{eff})\left(\dfrac{\partial u}{\partial x}+\dfrac{\partial v}{\partial y}+\dfrac{\partial w}{\partial z}\right)\right]+\dfrac{\partial}{\partial x}\left((\mu_{eff})\dfrac{\partial u}{\partial z}\right)$ $+\dfrac{\partial}{\partial y}\left((\mu_{eff})\dfrac{\partial v}{\partial z}\right)+\dfrac{\partial}{\partial z}\left((\mu_{eff})\dfrac{\partial w}{\partial z}\right)$
κ	$\dfrac{\mu_{eff}}{\sigma_\kappa}$	$P+G-\rho\varepsilon$
ε	$\dfrac{\mu_{eff}}{\sigma_\varepsilon}$	$\dfrac{\varepsilon}{\kappa}c_1 P+\dfrac{\varepsilon}{\kappa}c_3\max(G,0)-c_2\rho\dfrac{\varepsilon^2}{\kappa}$
h	$\dfrac{\mu_{eff}}{\sigma_h}$	S_{rad}

BOUNDARY CONDITIONS

For the cavity boundary walls, the no-slip condition on the velocity components has been applied. The derivatives of the turbulent kinetic energy κ is equated to zero, while the dissipation rate ε is evaluated from an empirical equation [5]. The temperature at the concrete surfaces was calculated using an energy balance of the incoming and outgoing heat fluxes at the boundaries by assuming adiabatic condition. For the fire shutter surfaces, the net heat fluxes are balanced by the convective and radiative heat gains or losses.

The conventional logarithmic wall functions are applied to all the solid boundaries for the momentum equation.

COMPUTATIONAL PROCEDURE

The conservation equations were discretized using the finite volume method. A hybrid differencing scheme was employed for the convection terms. The velocity and pressure linkage was achieved by the SIMPLEC algorithm. The discretization equations were solved using Stone's procedure. However, the Preconditioned Conjugate gradient method was employed for the pressure correction to accelerate convergence.

The non-uniform Cartesian grid is employed for all simulations with the grid concentrated in the vicinity of the solid boundary walls. A two-dimensional grid consisting of 40 cells across the width and 200 cells along the height, a total of 8000 cells, is adopted. Although in the current study a 2-D approach has been used, the FIRE3D is actually fully-featured for 3-D fire and flame spread simulations over a range of solid combustible materials from wood to PMMA with pyrolysis models incorporated.

RESULTS AND DISCUSSIONS

Computations for various combinations of emissivities and width of the gap between the fire shutters had been carried out using the FIRE3D package with the above mentioned parameters. It is found that for all simulation cases, of the steady states are reached at a time around 1000 seconds which is far less than the stipulated heat isolation time in BS476: Part 20. Therefore, in this article the steady state results which correspond to the highest temperature rise at the unexposed side are presented, although transient temperature and velocity fields were recorded for monitoring purposes during the processes of the simulations.

Figure 2 shows the temperature distribution at the surface of the fire shutter at the unexposed side with an emissivity of 0.02 and the width of the gap of 200, 276, 350, 400, and 500 mm. The curves indicate that in all cases the temperature increases with the height. This is due to the buoyancy driven re-circulating flows which contribute to the heat transfer across the air-cavity. It is worthy to note that the curves for different widths almost overlap one another. It could be inferred that the effects on the temperature rise and hence the heat transfer from the exposed to unexposed side due to the variation of the width are insignificant. Table 2 gives the average and maximum temperature and the rise at the unexposed face. With increase in width of the gap from 200 to 500 mm, the average temperature increases extremely slowly from 135.42 to 137.56°C, while the maximum temperature is found to decrease moderately from 220.35 to 194.88°C. These observations will be explained later with the use of the velocity field plots in Figures 3 to 7.

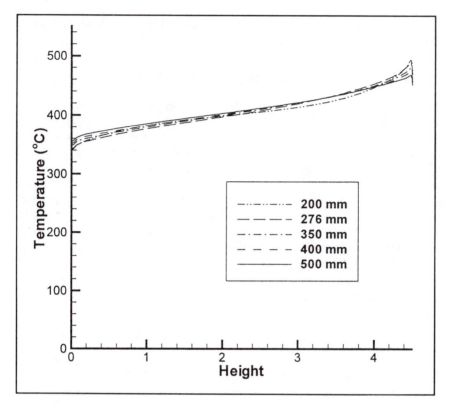

Figure 2. Steady-state temperature distribution on the fire shutter at the unexposed side with an emissivity of 0.02 and the air-cavity widths of 200, 276, 350, 400, and 500 mm.

Figure 8 shows the temperature distribution at the surface of the fire shutter at the unexposed side with various emissivity from 0.02 to 0.2 with the width of the gap of 276 mm. The temperature distribution curve shifts significantly upwards with the increasing emissivity. This indicates that the heat transfer rate is higher for larger emissivity. Also, the radiation heat transfer plays a predominant role in the overall heat transfer from the exposed to unexposed side fire shutters. It is also observed that the curves become "flatter" as the emissivity approaches the value of 0.2. This again confirms that in the case with large emissivity the heat transfer are substantially due to the radiation exchange where the convective heat transfer are relatively less insignificant. Table 3 shows the average and maximum temperature and the rise at the unexposed face for these cases. With the increase in emissivity, the average temperature increases substantially from 135.90 to 417.30°C and the maximum temperature increases from 216.32 to 448.73°C.

Table 2. The Steady-State Average and Maximum Temperature (Rise)
at the Unexposed Face for an Emissivity of 0.02
at Various Widths of Gap

Width of gap, mm (Separation)	Unexposed Side Temperature, °C	
	Average (Rise)	Maximum (Rise)
200	135.42 (110.42)	220.35 (195.35)
276	135.90 (110.90)	216.32 (191.32)
350	136.36 (111.36)	206.53 (181.53)
400	136.81 (111.81)	201.25 (176.25)
500	137.67 (112.67)	194.88 (169.88)

Figures 3 to 7 show plots of the temperature contours and velocity fields for the cases where the emissivity is 0.02 and the width of gap ranges from 200 to 500 mm.

From the velocity field plots given in Figures 3 to 7, velocities are found to increase generally with increase of the widths of the gap between the fire shutters. In other words, the wider the air-cavity, the faster is the re-circulation flowrate. This is due to the fact that less wall friction is effectively transmitted to the flow field. The increase in re-circulation flowrate results in a slight increase in the convective heat transfer as the cavity becomes wider. Hence, average temperature rise at the unexposed side is found to increase when the width is increased from 200 to 500 mm, as reported in Table 1. From the temperature contour plots in Figures 3 to 7, the increase in re-circulation flowrate also leads to stronger shearing of the temperature contours inside the cavity as width increases from 200 to 500 mm. This promotes effective mixing of the air inside the cavity and thus lowers the maximum temperature rise at the unexposed side as reported in Table 1.

From the above observations and discussions, in the design of double fire shutters assembly for the isolation of heat transfer from a fire compartment, the following essential criteria may be inferred:

1. The most significant factor governing heat transfer is the emissivity of the materials used for the fire shutters. The higher the emissivity the larger is the heat transfer and hence the temperature rise at the unexposed side.
2. Increase in width of the gap of the air-cavity seems to play a relatively minor role in the overall heat transfer and temperature rise at the unexposed side.
3. There is a trend toward increasing convective and hence the overall heat transfer as well as the average temperature rise at the unexposed side with

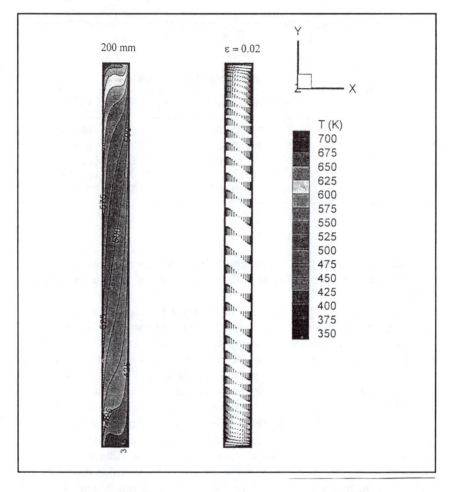

Figure 3. Steady-state temperature contours and velocity field in the air-cavity with a width of 200 mm and emissivity of 0.02.

increasing width of the gap due to the strengthening of the re-circulation air flow in the cavity. However, such a portion of heat transfer due to the convection is still far less significant in terms of order of magnitude than is the radiation heat transfer even at larger widths of the gap.

4. The maximum temperature rise at the unexposed side decreases with increase in width. This is because the air mixing is more efficient as the width increases.

To satisfy the requirement of heat isolation equivalent to that of BS476: Part 20, the average temperature rise should not exceed 140°C from the initial temperature

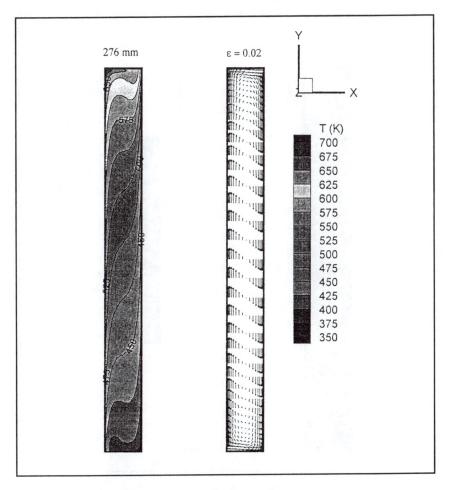

Figure 4. Steady-state temperature contours and velocity field in the air-cavity with a width of 276 mm and emissivity of 0.02.

within the stipulated fire resisting period, while the maximum temperature rise must be below 180°C. From the results presented above, this can only be achieved by having the double fire shutters assembly with an emissivity of less than 0.02. From Table 1, the reasonable range of width satisfying the criteria is 400 to 500 mm which gives an average and maximum temperature rise at the unexposed side of 111.81 to 112.67°C and 176.25 to 169.88°C respectively. The practical width will depend on the installation details as well as the thickness of the compartment wall.

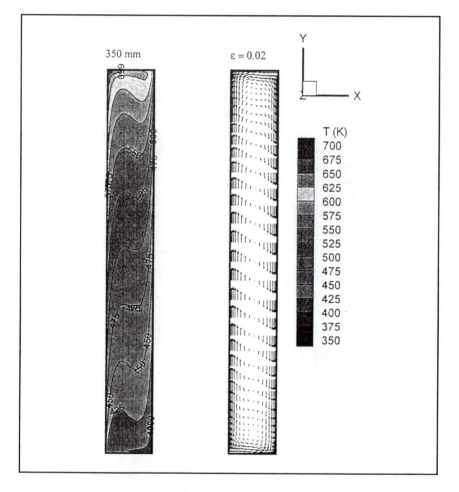

Figure 5. Steady-state temperature contours and velocity field in the air-cavity with a width of 350 mm and emissivity of 0.02.

CONCLUDING REMARKS

The CFD techniques applied have successfully demonstrated that the design of a double fire shutter system for the isolation of heat transfer from a fire compartment can be achieved. The most predominant factor affecting the heat isolation is the emissivity which is affected by the selection of materials for the fire shutters and their surface finishes. The overall heat transfer and temperature rise at the unexposed side are found notably increased with the increase in the emissivity. However, the width of the gap of the air-cavity between the double fire shutters

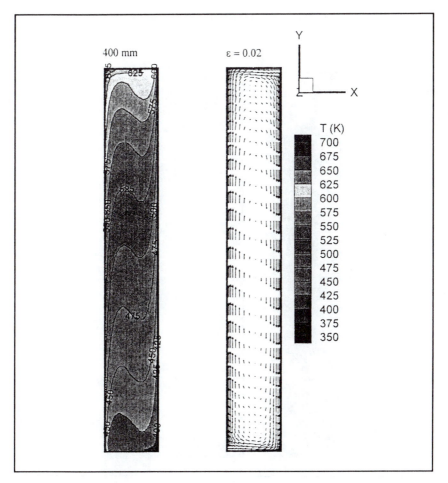

Figure 6. Steady-state temperature contours and velocity field in the
air-cavity with a width of 400 mm and emissivity of 0.02.

plays an insignificant role, if any, to the overall heat transfer and temperature at
the unexposed side. A clear yet moderate trend of increase of the temperature
rise has been observed with the increase in the width of the gap. In conclusion,
to isolate efficiently the heat transfer from a fire compartment to an acceptable
level, it is necessary that the fire shutters used by made of highly polished
metallic sheet such as stainless steel with mirror-type surface finish. However,
this could mean very special manufacturing processes and workmanship resulting
in very substantial increases in materials and manufacturing costs for adopting
such a design.

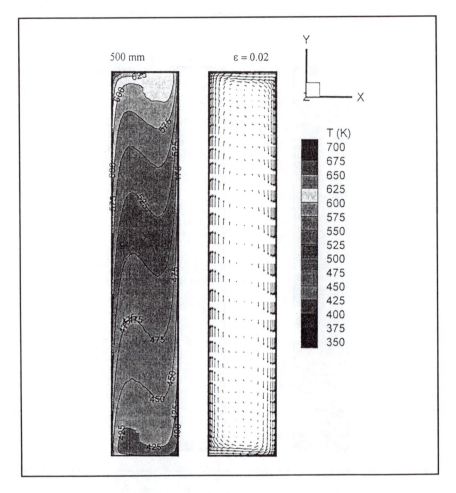

Figure 7. Steady-state temperature contours and velocity field in the
air-cavity with a width of 500 mm and emissivity of 0.02.

Further exploration could be made to look for alternatives using the CFD
techniques. The consideration of employing water spraying actuated automat-
ically by smoke detectors has been investigated. This may open up the possibility
of designing double fire shutters assemblies incorporating water spraying to serve
the same heat isolation objectives where ordinary mild sheet metal fire shutters
can be used at a relatively lower material and manufacturing cost.

The double fire shutters system will be installed in a multi-story factory building. Field tests are planned for comparison with computational results.

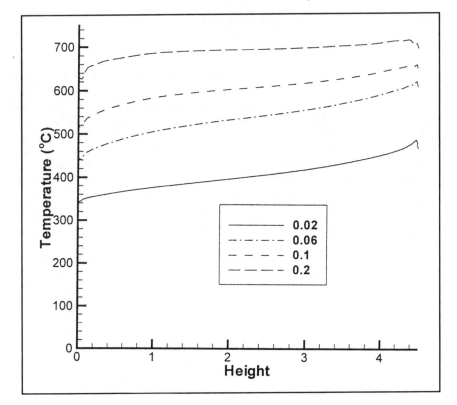

Figure 8. Steady-state temperature distribution on the fire shutter at the unexposed side for the width of gap of the air-cavity of 276 mm and emissivity of 0.02, 0.06, 0.1, and 0.2

Table 3. The Steady-State Average and Maximum Temperature (Rise) at the Unexposed Face for a Width Gap of 276 mm with Various Emissivities

Emissivity	Unexposed Side Temperature, °C	
	Average (Rise)	Maximum (Rise)
0.02	135.90 (110.90)	216.32 (191.32)
0.06	265.13 (240.13)	351.73 (326.73)
0.10	329.88 (304.88)	390.84 (365.84)
0.20	417.30 (392.30)	448.73 (423.73)

REFERENCES

1. *The Code of Practice on Fire Resisting Construction,* Buildings Department, Hong Kong Government, 1996.
2. *The Approved Document B, Building Regulations,* Department of the Environment, HMSO, United Kingdom, 1992.
3. A. S. Jamaluddin and P. J. Smith, Predicting Radiative Transfer in Rectangular Enclosures Using the Discrete Ordinates Method, *Combustion Science and Technology, 59,* pp. 321-340, 1988.
4. T. K. Kim and H. Lee, Effect of Anisotropic Scattering on Radiative Heat Transfer in Two-Dimensional Rectangular Enclosure, *International Journal of Heat and Mass Transfer, 31,* pp. 1711-1721, 1988.
5. B. E. Launder and D. B. Spalding, *Mathematical Models of Turbulence,* Academic Press, London, 1972.

CHAPTER 10

Spalling of High Strength Concrete at Elevated Temperatures

F. A. Ali, R. Connolly, P. J. E. Sullivan

The chapter describes work carried out by research workers world wide on spalling of high strength concrete at elevated temperatures. Spalling of high strength concrete depends on a number of factors including material properties, rate and form of heating, boundary conditions, geometrical, and environmental factors. Spalling is exacerbated by an increase in strength of concrete.

The use of high strength concrete in the construction of buildings within the United Kingdom is set to increase over future years, not least because of the significant potential for savings in construction costs, particularly for tall structures. However, there has been some concern about the performance of high strength concrete on exposure to fire and in particular its susceptibility to spalling. Spalling is the process of disintegration of a concrete's surface on exposure to heat and its occurrence can severely limit the fire resistance rating of concrete members. The objective of this chapter is to determine whether high strength concrete is at an increased risk of spalling.

A review of the literature has concluded that increasing concrete strength increases the probability of spalling and accordingly high strength concrete can be expected to demonstrate reduced performance at elevated temperatures. The probability of spalling of high strength concrete is particularly high when further unfavorable factors are present. Such unfavorable factors have been identified. Some of these factors cannot be controlled through design and thus the risk of spalling will always be present in high strength concrete unless some special preventative measures are put in place. Further work is necessary to identify such preventative measures. In addition, quantitative guidance is necessary on the design approach to controlling unfavorable factors such as curing and drying conditions, aggregate size and type, and concrete permeability.

INTRODUCTION

A large number of studies have been carried out on the performance of normal strength concrete at high temperatures over many years. A major finding of these studies has been the observed susceptibility of concrete to spalling on exposure to transient high temperatures. There are several distinct categories of spalling including surface spalling, corner spalling, aggregate spalling, and explosive spalling.

Although the different types of spalling vary in their severity, they each can cause damage and deterioration of concrete structures in fires and can limit the application of fire resistant design techniques to concrete. Explosive spalling is a particularly dangerous type of failure and its consequences can be catastrophic. Apart from potential injury and loss of life, explosive spalling can affect the integrity and stability of a concrete structure and is capable of precipitating total structural collapse.

The exposure of concrete to fire can create high temperature gradients and associated stresses. The elevated temperatures also initiate vaporization of both free and combined water within the concrete. While some of the resulting vapor escapes, more of it is contained within the gel pores and, with further addition of heat, increases in pressure occur. This build-up of pore pressure induces stresses within the gel structure. The magnitude of these stresses mainly depends on the rate of heating, the strength of the pore structure, and the permeability of the concrete. The thermal stresses and the pore pressure stresses combine to increase the strain energy within the gel pores of the concrete. If the gel pore structure is weak and permeable and a crack appears, the pressure is relieved and strain energy released. However, if the gel pore structure is strong and impermeable, strain energy can build up to very high levels with increasing temperatures. The sudden failure of the material matrix (due to a local weakness), can release the strain energy locally which may be followed by a chain reaction in the adjacent areas causing violent disruption of the concrete and explosive spalling.

Within the second half of this century it has been found economical to utilize concrete of a higher strength ($\geq$ 70 MPa) in construction, as use of higher strengths enables structural elements to carry more loads for a given size. High strength concrete is produced by using low water/cement ratios and super-plasticizing additives or similar agents. The strength can be increased to over 200 MPa by inclusion of silica fume and special aggregates. Although there has been considerable research on the behavior of high strength concrete in general, as Figure 1 shows relatively little work has focused on its performance at elevated temperatures. Simple extrapolation of data gathered for normal strength concrete to higher strength can be misleading and may even be dangerous.

The objective of this chapter is to review previous experimental research in order to investigate whether high strength concrete is more susceptible to spalling than normal strength concrete. The article will include a brief analysis of the influence of various factors on the occurrence of spalling.

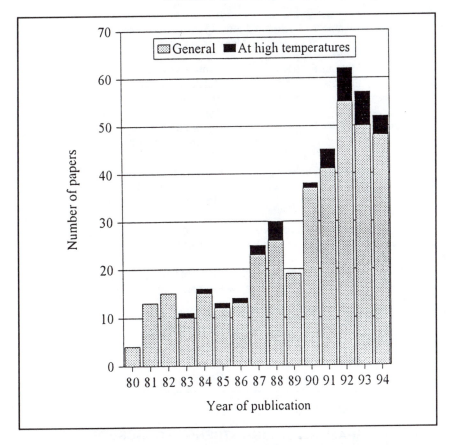

Figure 1. Bar chart of research on high strength concrete (1980-1994).

SPALLING OF NORMAL STRENGTH CONCRETE

The spalling of normal strength concrete at high temperatures has been investigated widely in different countries over the last sixty years by many researchers [1-12]. These studies have enabled the factors that influence the susceptibility of concrete to spalling to be identified as shown in Table 1.

Some of the above factors such as age, heating, and element type can be considered as uncontrollable, i.e., factors that cannot be controlled or adjusted by designers to minimize the probability of spalling.

In order to study the influence of some of these factors on the susceptibility of concrete to spalling an analysis of the available literature was undertaken. A summary of the results is shown in Table 2 which includes references to the literature indicating the source of the opinions presented where judgment can be made regarding the influence of different factors on spalling.

Table 1. Factors Influencing the Susceptibility
of a Concrete Member to Spalling

Material Property Factors	Compressive strength
	Moisture content
	Permeability
	Porosity
	Aggregate details
	Water/Cement ratio
Heating Factors	Rate of heating
	Nature of heating
	Maximum temperature
Boundary Conditions	Loading
	Restraint
Geometrical Factors	Element type
	Element size
Environmental Factors	Curing condition
	Drying condition
Other Factors	Age
	Cracking

SPALLING OF HIGH STRENGTH CONCRETE

Previous Experimental Studies

A great deal of work has been performed on the behavior of high strength concrete in the last fifty years. Only a few of these studies (the last 15 years) have investigated high strength concrete performance during fire (see Figure 1) and even fewer have recorded spalling under high temperatures.

One of the earliest studies on high strength concrete behavior under high temperatures was performed by Hertz in 1984 who performed an investigation of high strength (60-200 MPa) concrete cylinders (200 ö 100mm) [13] Hertz exposed the specimens to the relatively slow heating rate of 1ÉC/min up to a maximum temperature of 650ÉC. The moisture content of the concrete varied between 1.2 to 3 percent (by weight). Explosive spalling took place in 33 percent of the tested cylinders. It was concluded that high strength concrete may explode at slow rates of heating. In 1986, Hertz carried out another series of tests on concrete cylinders of the same size, but of normal strengths (40-70 MPa), exposing them to heating rates between 1 and 5°C/min. None of these exploded or spalled [14].

Table 2. Factors that Influence Concrete Spalling at High Temperatures

Factor	Cause	Effect on Susceptibility to Spalling [by Reference]
Compressive strength	Increased	More susceptible [5, 14, 18, 21]
Age	Older	More susceptible [10]
		Less susceptible [1, 4, 5, 6]
Moisture content	Increased	More susceptible [3, 4, 6, 9, 19]
Aggregate size	Increased	More susceptible [3, 5, 8]
Water/Cement ratio	Higher	More susceptible [5, 10]
Rate of heating	Higher	More susceptible [1, 3, 5, 10]
Nature of heating	Two sided	More susceptible [5, 6]
Applied load	Imposition	More susceptible [3, 5, 6, 9, 12, 17]
Restraint	Imposition	More susceptible [5]
Element thickness	Increased	Less susceptible [2, 5, 6, 7, 9, 17]
Curing	Water curing	More susceptible [1, 5]
Cracking	Presence	Less susceptible [5, 10, 18]

In 1985, Williamson and Rashed heated concrete cubes of strengths ranging from 41 to 121 MPa containing different amounts of silica fume [15]. The specimens were exposed to constant temperatures 20°C, 320°C, 520°C, and 700°C. No spalling was recorded in either the normal or high strength concrete specimens. An important conclusion of the study was that the loss of compressive strength at elevated temperatures was greater for high strength concrete containing silica fume than for concrete without silica fume.

Shirley et al. performed tests on high strength 900 × 900 × 100 mm concrete slabs [16]. The slabs were heated on one face only, in accordance with ASTM-E119 time-temperature regime. The slabs were fabricated using four high strength concretes (69-117 MPa) and one normal strength concrete (55 MPa). No spalling was observed in any slab and the study concluded that the fire resistance of normal and high strength concrete was not significantly different.

A study by Castillo and Durrani demonstrated that the imposition of axial loads on high strength concrete increases its susceptibility to spalling [17]. During experimental research on normal strength (31-63 MPa) and high strength concrete (89 MPa) cylinders, violent explosive spalling was recorded only in high strength concrete specimens loaded to 40 percent of their cold compressive strength. Unloaded specimens of both concrete types did not spall.

Arguably, the strongest evidence that high strength concrete are more susceptible to spalling than normal strength concrete was obtained by Sanjayan and Stocks [18]. They exposed two realistically sized T-beams to fire according to time-temperature curve AS 1530.4. One beam was fabricated from normal strength concrete (27 MPa) and the other from high strength concrete (105 MPa). The high strength concrete T-beam explosively spalled after eighteen minutes at 128°C (concrete temperature) while the normal strength concrete remained stable. They concluded that:

- High strength concrete is more prone to explosive spalling than normal strength concrete.
- The presence of cracks reduces the possibility of explosive spalling.
- Large concrete covers increase the possibility of concrete exploding.

Furumura et al. tested normal (29-45 MPa) and high strength (66 MPa) concrete 50 × 100 mm cylinders under constant temperatures ranging from 100°C to 700°C [19]. The temperatures were raised at the rate of 1°C/min. The cylinders were axially loaded as the authors intended to obtain the stress-strain curve of concrete at high temperatures. The samples were tested at different ages and the oldest was 1.5 years old. Furumura et al. did not observe spalling in any of the concrete tested.

Tachibana et al. reported surface spalling during fire tests on high strength concrete (88 MPa) [20]. Two realistically sized walls (1200 × 1200 × 150 mm) were heated at a rate of approximately 35°C/min. Two types of coarse aggregates were used; crushed hard sandstone and crushed quartz schist. Surface spalling was observed over 100 percent of the surface of the slab containing crushed quartz schist and over only 40 percent of the slab containing crushed hard sandstone.

Nishida et al. reported explosive spalling of high strength (103 MPa) concrete column [21]. The 300 × 300 × 1200 mm column was axially loaded with 25 percent of its compressive strength. Details of the reviewed experimental studies are summarized in Table 3, which contains useful data regarding the grouping of factors discussed earlier. The absence of some information in Table 3 is due to lack of data reported in the authors' papers. Table 3 allows quick comparison, analysis and conclusions regarding the importance of various factors.

Measures to Prevent Explosive Spalling

Two different approaches to the elimination of explosive spalling were those examined by Hertz [13] and Nishida et al. [21].

The approach used by Hertz depended on increasing the concrete's tensile strength using steel fibers. When he tested 200 × 100 mm, 100 × 50 mm and 52 × 28 mm high strength concrete cylinders reinforced with steel fibers, he observed that samples with larger amounts of fibers exploded while others did not. He concluded that using steel fibers was ineffective in reducing the risk of spalling and that concrete specimens with a high fiber content were, in fact, more likely to explode.

A different approach was adopted by Nishida et al. who included poly-propylene fibers in the concrete. These fibers melt at a temperature of approximately 150°C leaving "artificial capillaries" through which water vapor can escape reducing any vapor induced stresses. The authors tested high strength reinforced concrete columns prepared with and without polypropylene fibers. These columns were axially and eccentrically loaded up to 25 percent of its compressive strength. The tests revealed that using such fibers could significantly reduce the probability of spalling, as columns with polypropylene fibers did not explode while those without fibers exploded. Later, the authors confirmed their conclusions with tests on five meter high concrete columns. More details of these tests are reported in Table 3.

Discussion

There is no clear evidence that the increase in concrete strength is enough in itself to cause explosive spalling. Hertz [13], Williamson and Rashed [15], Shirley et al. [16], Castillo and Durrani [17] (unloaded samples), and Furumura et al. [19] did not report spalling of high strength concrete exposed to high temperatures. For an increase in concrete strength to cause spalling, it needs to be coincident with one or more of the factors identified as unfavorable in Table 2.

For example, when Castillo and Durrani tested normal and high strength concrete samples no explosive spalling was recorded. But when they imposed axial loads, high strength concrete samples exploded violently while the normal strength loaded samples did not. Here the strength factor caused spalling only when it was accompanied by the loading factor. The reason that the authors mentioned did not observe spalling of high strength concrete was that the additional unfavorable factor of imposed loading was absent.

As many unfavorable factors exist in practice, an increase in concrete strength is often quite sufficient to precipitate spalling on exposure to fire. Strong evidence supporting this hypothesis is provided by the work of Sanjayan and Stocks [18], who recorded explosive spalling when they held the unfavorable factors constant and increased the concrete strength.

The successful approach to eliminate explosive spalling used by Nishida et al. [21] is not fully understood, but is thought to be related to the introduction of "artificial channels" at high temperatures through which vapor can escape. In practice, similar channels can develop in the form of load induced cracks. Cracks typically start to develop in flexural members such as beams, slabs, and eccen-trically loaded columns during the early stages of load, i.e., where the applied moment is in the order of 25 percent of the ultimate moment capacity of the concrete section. It would thus be useful to observe the incidence of spalling in flexural members in order to further assess the validity of the "artificial channel" hypothesis.

Table 3. Details of Previous Experimental Studies Performed on
High Strength Concrete under High Temperatures

| Reference | Geometrical Factors | | | Heating Factors | | |
	Specim. Type	Dim. cm	Thick cm	Heat Rate °C/min	Max. temp. °C	Side of Heat
1	2	3	4	5	6	7
Hertz D. [13,14] Denmark (1984-1992)	Cylinder	10	20	1	150-650	all
	Cylinder	10	20	1	200-600	all
	Cylinder	5.7	10	1	600	all
	Cylinder	2.8	5.2	1	600	all
	Cylinder	20	10	1-5	600	all
Williamson et al. [15] USA, 1985	Cube	5 × 5	5	10	700	all
Shirley et al. [16] USA, 1988	Slab	90 × 90	10.2	ASTM	1316	one
	Slab	90 × 90	10.2	=	1316	one
Castillo et al. [17] USA, 1990	Cylinder	5.1	10.2	7-8	800	all
	Cylinder	5.1	10.2	7-8	800	all
Sanjayan et al. [18] Australia, 1994	T-beam	120 × 25 × 45 × 250L	20-15	AS1530	1100	all
	T-beam	120 × 25 × 45 × 250L	20-15	AS1530	1100	all
Furumura et al. [19] Japan, 1993	Cylinder	5	10	1	700	all
	Cylinder	5	10	1	700	all
Tachibana et al. [20] Japan, 1994	Wall	120 × 120	15	35	925	one
	Wall	120 × 120	15	35	925	one
Nishida et al. [21] Finland, 1994	Column	25 × 25	100	—	—	all
	Column	25 × 25	100	—	—	all
	Column	25 × 25	100	—	—	all
	Column	25 × 25	100	—	—	all
	Column	50 × 40	559	DIN102	—	all
	Cylinder	15	30	14-25	750	all

Key: HSC = high strength concrete, NSC = normal strength concrete, b.b. = burned bauxite, rh = relative humidity, ls = lime stone, c.q.s = crushed quartz schist, c.h.s = crushed hardstone, c.g. = crushed gravel, e = eccentrically loaded, SF = steel fibers, PF = polypropylene fibers, s.w. = self weight, L = tee beam length, w = by weight.
*All spalling temperatures are concrete temperatures, except Hertz tests.

	Material Properties Factors				Bound Factor	
Comp. Strength MPa	Moist. Cont. %	Curing Cond.	Agg. Type	Age (days)	Load. Level f_o/f_c'	Comments
8	9	10	11	12	13	14
64-207	1.2-3% w.	water	—	80	0	HSC without SF, ≈ 40% of cylinders spalled at 350-650°C. (silica fume used)
82-207	—	—	—	—	—	HSC with SF, ≈ 16% of cylinders spalled at 400-600°C. (silica fume used) HSC without SF, No spalling HSC without SF, No spalling
80-168	—	—	b.b	—	0	HSC without SF, No spalling
77-192	—	—	b.b	—	0	
40-70	—	—	b.b	—	0	
44-121	—	water	—	28	0	HSC with silica fume, No spalling
69-117	77 rh	moist.	ls	77-130	0	Four HSC with slabs tested, No spalling. (only two slabs are with silica fume)
55	84 rh	moist.	ls	113	0	One NSC slab, No spalling
89	—	moist.	ls	90	0.4	HSC spalled at 320-360°C
31-63	—	moist.	ls	65-90	0.4	NSC, No spalling (similar tests on unloaded samples, No spalling)
105	4.6	—	—	105	s.w	HSC spalled at 128°C
27	4	—	—	105	s.w	NSC, No spalling (no spalling at cracked parts)
29-45	—	water	c.g	180-300	0-100	NSC, No spalling
66	—	water	c.g	420-510	0-100	HSC, No spalling
87.3	4.25	moist.	c.h.s	—	0	40% surface spalling at 221°C
87.9	3.80	moist.	c.q.s.	—	0	100% surface spalling at 279°C
102.9	4.21w	moist.	—	27	0.50	HSC without PF, spalled after 6 min.
103	4.4w	moist.	—	133	0.50	HSC with PF, Minor spalling
89.5	4.62w	moist.	—	90	0.57	HSC with PF, No spalling
89.5	4.62w	moist.	—	90	0.57e	HSC with PF, No spalling
117.3	3.72w	moist.	—	53	0.5	HSC with PF, local spalling
103	4.4w	—	—	133	0.3-0.4	HSC with PF, No spalling

CONCLUSIONS

1. The occurrence of explosive spalling severely reduces the fire resistance of concrete.
2. Increasing concrete strength increases the probability of spalling and accordingly high strength concrete can be expected to demonstrate reduced performance at elevated temperatures.
3. The probability of spalling of high strength concrete is particularly high when further unfavorable factors are present.
4. Such unfavorable factors have been identified and some of them may be avoided through design. Other factors remain outside of the control of the designer and thus the risk of spalling will always be present in high strength concrete unless some special preventative measures are put in place.
5. Further work is necessary to identify such preventative measures, which might include use of steel fibers, polypropylene fibers or air entertainment. Furthermore, some quantitative guidance is required on the control through design of unfavorable factors such as curing and drying conditions, aggregate size and type, and concrete permeability.

Research work is being carried out at the City University under the supervision of the third author to study the principal factors affecting explosive spalling of high strength concrete at fire temperatures.

REFERENCES

1. A. A. Akhtaruzzaman and P. J. E. Sullivan, Explosive Spalling of Concrete Exposed to High Temperature, *Proceedings of the International Conference on Structural Mechanics in Reactor Technology, Berlin,* 4H, pp. 57-69, 1971
2. L. A. Ashton and N. Davey, Investigations of Building Fires—Part 5, *National Building Studies Research Paper 12,* HMSO, London, 1953.
3. V. N. Bogoslovski and V. M. Roitman, Explosive Failure of Concrete in Fire, *Beton I Zhelzobeton, 24*:6, pp. 39-41, 1978.
4. A. Christiaanse, A. Langhorst, and A. Gerriste, *Discussion of Fire Resistance of Lightweight Concrete and Spalling,* Dutch Society of Engineers (STUVO), Report 12, Holland, 1971.
5. R. J. Connolly, *Spalling of Concrete in Fire,* Ph.D. thesis, University of Aston, Birmingham, April 1995.
6. W. J. Copier, The Spalling of Normal Weight and Light Weight Concrete Exposed to Fire, *Journal of The American Concrete Institute, 80*:4, pp. 352-353, 1983.
7. M. Hanneman and H. Thomas, *Resistance of Reinforced Concrete Elements and Floors in Fires,* In Deutscher Ausschub fur Stahlbeton 132, W. Ernest and Son, Berlin, 1959.
8. H. L. Malhotra, *Spalling of Concrete in Fires, Technical Report 118,* Construction Industry Research and Information Association, London, 1984.

9. C. Meyer-Ottens, *The Question of Spalling of Concrete Structural Elements of Standard Concrete under Fire Loading*, Ph.D. thesis, Technical University of Braunschweig, Germany, 1972.

10. K. D. Nekrasov, *Fire Resistance Concrete Moscow*, Strousdat, 1974.

11. Y. Sertmehemetoglu, *On a Mechanism of Spalling of Concrete under Fire Conditions*, Ph.D. thesis, Kings College, London, 1977.

12. V. V. Zhukov, *Explosive Failure of Concrete during a Fire*, proceedings Fire Resistant Concrete, Stroezdat, Moscow, 1970.

13. K. D. Hertz, *Heat Induced Explosion of Dense Concrete, Report No. 166*, Institute of Building Design Technology, University of Denmark, 1984.

14. K. D. Hertz, Danish Investigations on Silica Fume Concrete at Elevated Temperatures, *ACI Materials Journal, 89*:4, pp. 345-347, 1992.

15. R. B. Williamson and I. Rashed, *High Strength Concrete and Mortars in High Temperature Environments*, Proceeding of Materials Research Society Symposium, *42*, California, 1985.

16. T. Shirley, R. G. Burg, and A. E. Fiorato, Fire Endurance of High-Strength Concrete Slabs, *ACI Materials Journal, 85*:2, pp. 102-108, March-April 1988.

17. C. Castillo and A. J. Durrani, Effect of Transient High Temperature on High Strength Concrete, *ACI Materials Journal, 87*:1, January-February 1990.

18. G. Sanjayan and L. J. Stocks, Spalling of High-Strength Silica Fume Concrete in Fire, *ACI Materials Journal, 90*:2, March-April 1993.

19. F. Furumura, T. Ave, Y. Shinohara, K. Tomaturi, K. Kuroha, and I. Kokubo, *Mechanical Properties of High Strength Concrete at High Temperatures*, Report of the Research Laboratory of Engineering Materials Tokyo, Institute of Technology No. 187, Japan, 1993.

20. D. Tachibana, H. Kumagai, N. Yamazaki, and T. Suzuki, High Strength Concrete (fc=600Kgf/cm2) for Building Construction, *ACI Materials Journal, 9*:4, pp. 390-400, 1994.

21. A. Nishida, N. Yamazaki, H. Inque, U. Schneider and U. Diederichs, *Study on the Properties of High Strength Concrete with Short Polypropylene Fibres for Spalling Resistance*, International Symposium on Concrete under Severe Conditions, Sappero, Japan, p. 10, August 1995.

CHAPTER 11

The Effect of Char Oxidation on the Flaming Combustion Characteristics of Wood Materials

B. Moghtaderi, V. Novozhilov,
D. F. Fletcher, and J. H. Kent

In order to investigate the role of char oxidation on the flaming combustion characteristics of wood-based materials, a number of small-scale experiments were performed using a cone calorimeter. This has been motivated by the need to have realistic models of wood combustion for use in a Computational Fluid Dynamics (CFD) model of building fires. The results of this study indicate that for the case of a horizontal orientation the role of char oxidation on the overall combustion process is not significant and, hence, it can be ignored as far as the modeling of the flaming combustion is concerned. However, for the case of a vertical orientation the effect of char oxidation is relatively important and should be taken into account. For the species considered here, char oxidation accounted for approximately 10 percent of the heat release rate during the flaming combustion period. Although the study presented here is mainly concerned with wood-based materials, the results are equally applicable to other types of char-forming solid fuels.

Charring materials, like wood, constitute a substantial fraction of the fuel load in many building fires. For this reasoning an understanding of their behavior under high temperature burning conditions is crucial.

A general schematic of the different chemical processes involved in the burning of wood is shown in Figure 1. The figure identifies two distinct phases of the wood burning process: 1) pyrolysis which results in the liberation of volatiles and the formation of the char residue and 2) combustion that can proceed by two alternative pathways involving flaming combustion and glowing (smouldering) combustion. Flaming combustion occurs when, under certain conditions,

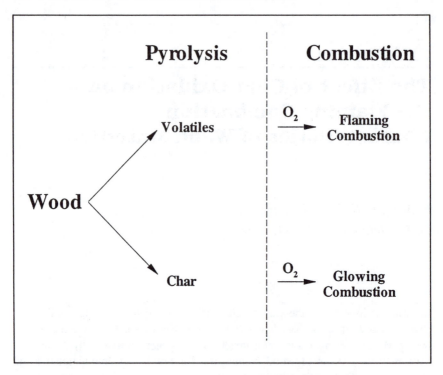

Figure 1. Schematic diagram of the chemical processes involved
in the burning of wood.

the volatiles react with the oxygen in the boundary layer and produce a stable
flame. Consequently, heat is released by the gas-phase combustion of volatile
products. A part of this heat is transferred back to the solid object to continue
the process.

Smouldering combustion takes place when the volatiles liberated from the
surface of the fuel are not in sufficient quantity for ignition, but enough heat is
generated to keep the fuel pyrolysing.

The effect of char oxidation on the characteristics of glowing combustion has
long been recognized and there are many research papers on this subject address-
ing different aspects of the problem. Kashiwagi and co-workers have measured
mass loss rates from white pine specimens at different levels of oxygen concentrations ranging between 0 and 21 percent [1, 2]. Their results showed that the
mass loss rate decreases by approximately 20 percent when the oxygen concentration decreases from 21 percent to 10.5 percent. For 0 percent oxygen
concentration the mass loss rate was found to be only 50 percent of its value for
the ambient oxygen concentration (21%). A similar study for Douglas fir was

carried out by Nurbakhsh [3]. His results show a 35 percent decrease in the mass loss rate between 21 percent and 0 percent oxygen concentration. According to these studies, for the glowing combustion of wood, char oxidation plays a controlling role in the overall combustion process.

However, based on the available literature, the effect of char oxidation on the characteristics of flaming combustion is somewhat less significant, mainly because in this mode of combustion the flame envelops the degrading solid and, hence, blocks the diffusion of oxygen toward the exposed surface of the solid [4]. In reality, however, the char layer does not maintain its original shape during the burning process. In fact, char layers shrink and have cracks and fissures. As a result, small jets of volatiles emerge from these cracks and fissures, disturbing the shape of the flame, thus providing a path for diffusion of oxygen to the char surface. Therefore, char oxidation occurs over the whole duration of the combustion process. The question is: "how significant is the effect of char oxidation on the overall combustion process?" This question has been addressed by a number of investigators but perhaps Janssens' work is most related to the present study [5].

This chapter presents the results of an experimental study that was performed to address the above question. It was motivated by the need to have realistic models of wood combustion that can be used as sub-models in a CFD model of fire spread and extinguishment.

EXPERIMENTAL

In this study, the NIST-type cone calorimeter was utilized and operated in accordance with the recommendations in ASTM E 1354-90 [6] and ISO/DIS 5660 [7]. The experiments were conducted on specimens of Pacific maple at various irradiance levels (20-85 kW/m^2) and for various orientations (horizontal and vertical).

All specimens were 100 mm square as required for testing in the cone calorimeter and the thickness of all samples was 19 mm. The samples were cut from one timber length to improve the consistency of the tests. Specimens were also oven-dried (at 105°C) in order to eliminate the effect of moisture content on the combustion process. Prior to testing, the unexposed surface and edges of each specimen were wrapped in aluminium foil (to reduce the edge effects) as specified in ISO/DIS 5660 [7], then laid on Kaowool mat within a 25 mm deep stainless steel tray to minimize the heat loss from the unexposed surface.

Measurements of the surface temperature were performed to characterize the behavior of the char layer. For this purpose, prior to drying, all samples were instrumented with 75 μm diameter chromel-alumel thermocouples in accordance with the method developed by Urbas [8]. This method, however, does not ensure that good contact is made between the thermocouples and the material after charring is initiated. Therefore, during the execution of the method, special care was taken to make sure that the thermocouples were in good contact with the surface.

Apart from the surface temperature, for each specimen the time to piloted ignition, heat release rate (HRR), weight loss, yield of the combustion products including CO and CO_2, heat of combustion (HOC), and oxygen depletion rate were measured during the test. A minimum of two runs were carried out for each orientation at each heat flux. If the runs were significantly different a third run was carried out.

RESULTS AND DISCUSSION

The general shape of the heat release rate (HRR) curve for a sample with finite thickness and an insulated back face consists of two peaks. Figure 2 shows such a HRR curve for a horizontal sample of Pacific maple at an irradiance of 25 kW/m^2. The heat of combustion (HOC), which is the ratio of the HRR to mass loss rate (MLR), is also shown in this Figure.

As can be seen in Figure 2, around the time of the second peak in the HRR curve, the HOC starts to rise rapidly. When the HRR curve decreases to its final value, the HOC reaches a more or less constant value of about 29 MJ/kg, which is close to the value of 31 MJ/kg reported in the literature [5] for the heat of combustion of char (carbon). This means that (for a sample with finite thickness) the effect of char oxidation for a horizontal orientation becomes significant only around the second peak which is close to the end of flaming period. This is supported by the fact that the surface temperature also exhibits an increase around the second peak of the mass loss rate curve, as shown in Figure 3. (Note that the sharp increase in the temperature at the end of the test is due to the fact that the thermocouple has been broken.) Similar results are also obtained for other levels of incident heat flux as can be seen in Figures 4 and 5.

Therefore, it can be concluded that char oxidation does not play a controlling role in the flaming combustion process of wood-based materials at least for the horizontal orientation. This is quite similar to what has been proposed by Janssens [5]. The implication of this finding regarding the mathematical model-ing of the wood burning process is that for all practical purposes (for finite size samples in the horizontal orientation) the effect of char oxidation during the flaming period can be neglected. However, the validity of this statement for the vertical orientation should also be investigated. In this regard, it is useful to describe the sequence of events which occur during the burning of a vertical wood specimen in the cone calorimeter.

Typically within 10-40 s after ignition, the first group of main fissures began to develop. Their orientation was always perpendicular to the grain direction. When the grain was vertical the fissures ran across the whole width of the specimen (see Figure 6a). In the case of horizontal grains, the fissures covered the whole height (see Figure 6b). Toward the end of each test, a few line fissures also

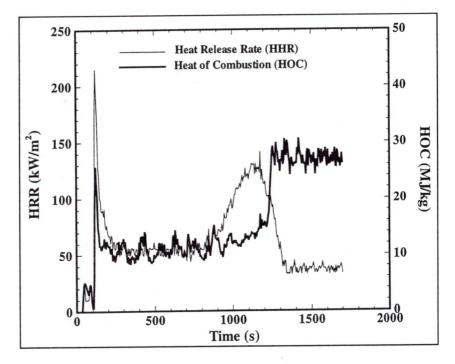

Figure 2. The *HRR* and *HOC* curves obtained for a horizontal sample of Pacific maple at an irradiance of 25 kW/m^2.

developed parallel to the grain. Typically the width of the main fissures increase from 2 mm at the beginning of the test to about 10 mm by the end of the test. (The depth of typical fissures varies between 5 to 15 mm.) At the beginning of each test the entire exposed surface of the specimen was covered by flames. However, as time passed and the fissures developed, the flames tended to emerge only from the fissures. From the fluid mechanics point of view this can be attributed to the fact that volatiles always flow along the path of least resistance.

In the case of horizontal fissures (vertical grain) the volatiles left the fissures and covered the surface above them with flames. Thus, during the intense burning period, all the area above the bottom fissure was covered by a flame sheet. As a result, the ambient oxygen could not reach the exposed surface and char oxidation could not occur. However, later in the test, as the main fissures broadened, the mass flow of volatiles near the bottom was not sufficient to support a flame. Hence, the lower boundaries of the flaming region moved slowly upward. Consequently, the lower part of the specimen was exposed to the air (see Figure 6a) and went through the char oxidation process. As a result, the surface temperature measured in the lower part of the specimen was higher than the one measured in

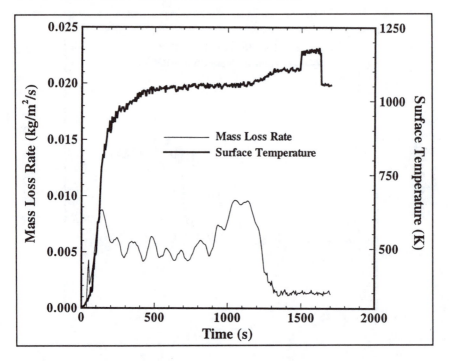

Figure 3. The mass loss rate and the surface temperature obtained for
a horizontal sample of Pacific maple at an irradiance of 25 kW/m².

the area covered by the flame sheet (see Figure 7). This is because under
the conditions of the experiment the rate of diffusion of oxygen to the flame
sheet is essentially the same as it is to the area exposed to air. Since the efficiency
of the heat transfer to the surface is greater for char oxidation than flaming
combustion, which takes place away from the surface [8], the temperatures of
the lower part of the specimens (outside the flame sheet) were observed to be
higher. The char oxidation process can also be identified visually since it is often
accompanied by a change in the surface color (from black to red) that can be
easily observed.

On the other hand, in the case of vertical fissures (horizontal grain) the flames
were contained within the fissures almost throughout the whole duration of the
test (see Figure 6b). As a consequence, the ambient oxygen could easily reach the
exposed areas and oxidize the char layer. Therefore, for the case of vertical
fissures, the char oxidation plays a more significant role on the overall combustion process.

For both types of fissures the flames were more intense toward the top edge of
the specimen because the mass flow of volatiles along the fissures increased with

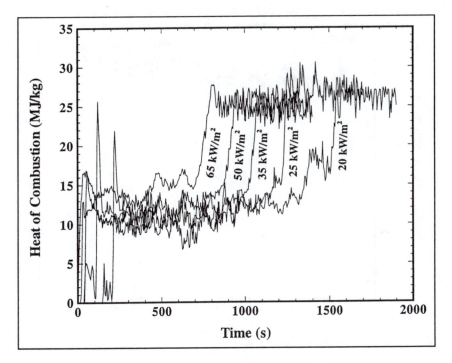

Figure 4. The effective heat of combustion as a function of the incident heat flux (horizontal orientation).

the height due to the cumulative contribution along the way [8]. At the end of the pyrolysis process all the flames disappeared and only a partially burnt char layer was left, since much of the char had already been consumed by oxidation. This is quite different from the observation made during the tests in the horizontal orientation. As Figure 2 indicates, after the flaming period the char oxidation process continued until nothing was left from the original solid except ash.

Based on the discussion presented in the foregoing section, it is expected that for the case of a vertical orientation the impact of char oxidation on the flaming combustion characteristics of wood-based materials would be quite significant. To quantify this effect a simply analysis is performed here using the data obtained from the experiments. As the first step, the effective heat of combustion (HOC$_{av}$) is defined as follows:

$$HOC_{av} = \frac{HRR_{av}}{MLR_{av}}$$

(1)

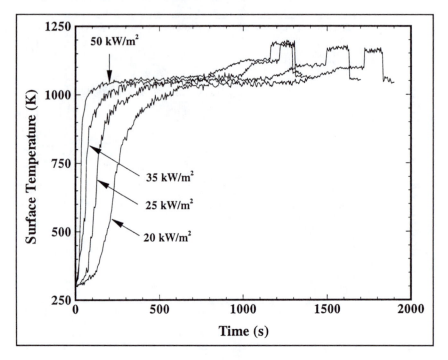

Figure 5. The surface temperature as a function of the incident
heat flux (horizontal orientation).

where HRR$_{av}$ and MLR$_{av}$ are the average values of the heat release and mass loss rates, respectively. All averages are calculated over the entire flaming period using data obtained from the experiments. Generally, for the horizontal specimens of Pacific maple, values of HRR are 28 percent higher than those obtained in the vertical orientation. (From a physical point of view, the higher HRR in the horizontal orientation can be attributed to the flame radiation which is significantly affected by the shape of the flame. As mentioned before, in the vertical orientation the gas-phase combustion occurs primarily above the upper edge of the sample. However in the horizontal orientation the flame takes a conical shape that has a much greater volume. This enhances the gas-phase combustion which in turn results in a higher level of radiative feedback to the sample.) On the contrary, there is no significant difference between the horizontal and vertical values of MLR$_{av}$ because regardless of the orientation, the material produces the same volatile yield. As a result one expects the effective heat of combustion for the vertical orientation to be about 28 percent lower than that of

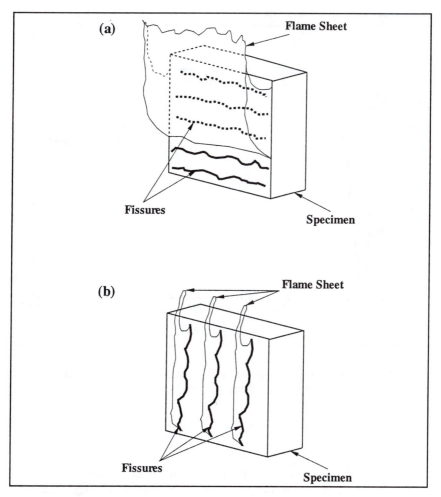

Figure 6. A schematic diagram of a burning sample of wood for the cases of: (a) horizontal fissures, (b) vertical fissures.

the horizontal orientation. In other words, the combustion efficiency for the horizontal orientation should be higher. This is a valid expectation, as Figure 8 indicates.

Now, if for each incident heat flux the corresponding value of HOC_{av} is multiplied by the one-minute average mass loss rate ($MLR_{1\ min}$), a good estimate of the one-minute average heat release rate ($HRR_{1\ min}$) must be obtained. (Note

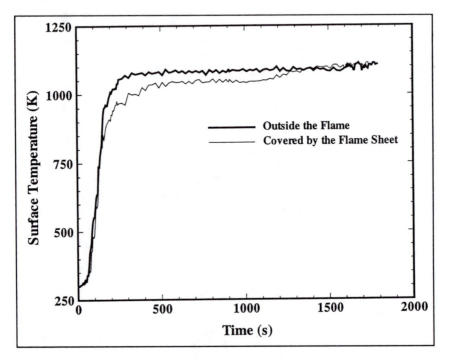

Figure 7. The surface temperature of a vertical Pacific maple sample
measured at two different locations.

that $HRR_{1\ min}$ is representative of the combustion process around the first peak
in the HRR curve [5] and this explains why its estimation is so important.) As
Figure 9 shows, that is correct for the horizontal orientation; however, in the case
of the vertical orientation the calculated values of $HRR_{1\ min}$ under-predict
the experimental curve by about 10 percent. This means that if the heat release
in the vertical orientation were only due to the combustion of volatiles, the
difference between the horizontal and vertical values of $HRR_{1\ min}$ would
have to be 38 percent (the difference between the calculated curves) not the
28 percent shown by the experimental data. Therefore, there must be another
source of heat release. Although a firm conclusion is very difficult to assert,
this difference can be attributed mainly to the char oxidation process which
is highly exothermic. Therefore, the effect of char oxidation on the flaming
combustion characteristics of wood-based materials in the vertical orientation
cannot be ignored. This is quite different to the statement made earlier about
the horizontal case.

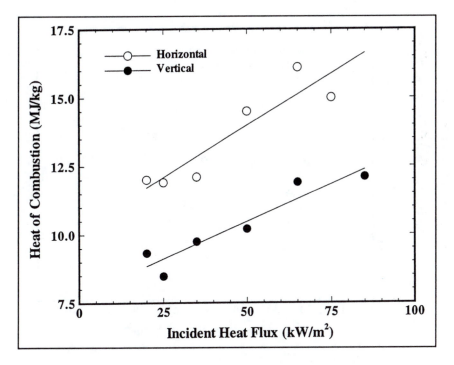

Figure 8. The effective heat of combustion of the horizontal and vertical specimens of Pacific maple as a function of the incident heat flux.

CONCLUSIONS

A series of small-scale experiments were performed on specimens of Pacific maple in the horizontal and vertical orientations using a cone calorimeter. The main objective was to investigate the effect of char oxidation on the flaming combustion characteristics of wood materials. This study led to the following major conclusions:

1. The impact of char oxidation on the overall combustion process of wood-based materials depends highly on the physical condition of the sample.
2. For finite size samples in a horizontal orientation the role of char oxidation on the overall combustion process is not significant and, hence, it can be ignored as far as the modeling of flaming combustion is concerned.
3. For the case of a vertical orientation the effect of char oxidation is relatively important and should be taken into account. For the species considered here, the char oxidation accounts for approximately 10 percent of the heat release rate during the flaming combustion period.

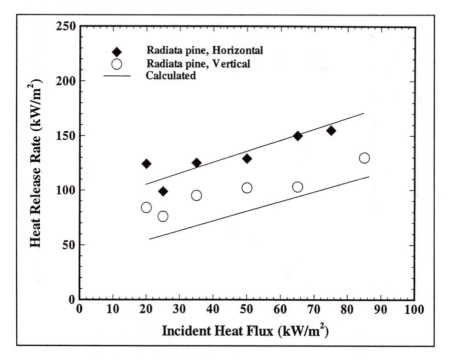

Figure 9. The one-minute average heat release rate of Pacific maple in
the horizontal and vertical orientations.

REFERENCES

1. T. Kashiwagi, T. J. Ohlemiller, and K. Werner, Effects of External Radiant Flux and Ambient Oxygen Concentration on Nonflaming Gasification Rates and Evolved Products of White Pine, *Combustion and Flame, 69*, pp. 331-345, 1987.
2. T. J. Ohlemiller, T. Kashiwagi, and K. Werner, Wood Gasification at Fire Level Heat Fluxes, *Combustion and Flame, 66*, pp. 155-170, 1987.
3. S. Nurbakhsh, *Thermal Decomposition of Charring Materials*, Ph.D. thesis, Michigan State University, East Lansing, 1989.
4. C. Di Blasi, Modelling and Simulation of Combustion Processes of Charring and Non-Charring Materials, *Prog. Energy Combustion Science, 19*, pp. 71-104, 1993.
5. M. Janssens, Rate of Heat Release of Wood Products, *Fire Safety Journal, 17*, pp. 217-238, 1991.

6. American Society for Testing and Materials, *Standard Test Method for Heat and Visible Smoke Release Rates for Materials and Products Using an Oxygen Consumption Calorimeter*, ASTM E 1354-90, 1990.

7. International Standard Organisation, *Rate of Heat Release from Building Products*, ISO/DIS 5660, 1991.

8. J. Urbas and W. J. Parker, Surface Temperature Measurements on Burning Wood Specimens in the Cone Calorimeter and the Effect of Grain Orientation, *Fire and Materials, 17*, pp. 205-208, 1993.

CHAPTER 12

Behavior of Plywood Lining in Full Scale Room Fire Tests

J. Zhang, T. J. Shields, G. W. H. Silcock,
and M. A. Azhakesan

A detailed study of the behavior of plywood wall lining was conducted in an ISO room enclosure fire. In addition to its contribution to fire growth, observations included ignition behavior, surface flame spread, and charring of the lining. For the corner fire scenario conducted in this study the linings responded differently in three distinctly different regions of each of adjacent walls, i.e., region I close to the fire source; region II at the ceiling and wall interface; and region III the remainder of the wall surface. In region I, ignition occurred over a relatively large area, resulting in a large pyrolysis front and rapid upward flame spread. In region II, convective heat flow preheated the lining surfaces but ignition was induced by a laterally advancing flame front. Region III was characterized by downward flame spread from region II while lateral flame spread from region I to region III was negligible. Ignition in region III was caused by the downward advancing flame front and a distinct linear pyrolysis front was apparent. The rate of flame spread increased with room temperatures. The data obtained suggest that the developed fire in regions I and II was not sufficient to cause flashover. When fire spread to region III, flashover rapidly ensued. The analysis of charring of the linings indicated two areas of severe burning, one directly in line with the source fire plume and the other at the boundary area between the ceiling and the wall, close to the fire corner location.

Combustible wall and ceiling linings are potential fire hazards in that once ignited, combustible linings may rapidly propagate fire, accelerate growth of an enclosure fire, and eventually contribute to the onset of flashover provided there is sufficient ventilation. Although the use of combustible linings in buildings has been controlled for many decades, the actual behavior of wall linings under real fire conditions has not been fully understood. Only limited information on the behavior of commonly used lining materials in full scale enclosure fire tests is available in the literature [1-4]. This chapter is presented as part of a program directed to the study of the growth and development of enclosure fires subjected to feedback from hot gases and from heat contributing by combustible wall linings under real fire conditions. Some initial results focusing on the behavior of plywood linings when the location of the fire is in a corner of the enclosure are discussed and analyzed.

EXPERIMENTAL CONDITIONS

A burn room constructed to ISO standard [5] and modified to include observation panels in the west wall was used in the experiments and is shown in Figure 1. The enclosure walls and the ceiling were made of concrete and insulated with 15 mm thick ceramic fiber boards. The north and east walls were partially covered with 19 mm thick untreated plywood linings of a density of 478 ± 29 kg m^{-3} while the remainder of the walls were covered with 12 mm thick gypsum plaster board as shown in Figure 2. The ceiling directly above the corner fire location was also lined with gypsum plaster board. Both the plywood lining and plaster board were conditioned at $23 \pm 2°C$ and relative humidity of 50 ± 5 percent for seventy-two hours before the testing.

The surface temperatures of the linings were measured using K type thermocouples, 1.5 mm in diameter, with the head of each thermocouple tightly contacting the lining surface. The locations of each of the thermocouples on the linings are shown in Figure 2. The remainder of the thermocouples were installed as suggested by the ISO 9705 standard [5].

The fuel used was mineralized methylated spirits consisting of 93 percent ethanol and 7 percent methanol in a 550 mm × 550 mm × 100 mm steel tray and located at the corner 50 mm away from the corner walls and 400 mm above the floor. Approximately 8 kg of the fuel was used for each test and mass loss was measured by a load cell installed beneath the tray. The average heat release rate measured in the cone calorimeter without external heat flux was 350 kW m^{-2} and thus the estimated average heat release from the fuel tray based on area unit was approximately 105 kW. Data were captured using a system capable of recording output from over 150 channels.

RESULTS AND DISCUSSION

Ignition

From an analysis of surface temperature measurements it was apparent that the ignition behaviors of the linings were different in three distinct regions. The relative positions of these regions are shown in Figure 3. The first was a narrow region extending from above the fuel to the surface of the ceiling. The initial

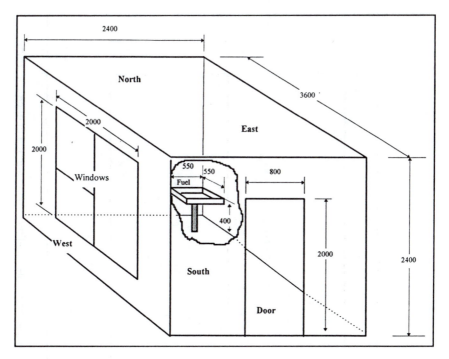

Figure 1. Schematic diagram of the fire test enclosure with dimensions (mm).

ignition occurred within an area of approximately 200 mm × 400 mm (width × height) at approximately 400 mm above the fuel surface after approximately a 190-second exposure to the flame plume. Following initial ignition, the extended flame plume caused ignition in a larger area at a higher position. It was observed that the pyrolysis front was an area front instead of a clearly delineated linear front, i.e., the area ignited was in close proximity to a flame plume from which flux incident to the lining was high, thus the likely ignition condition for upward surface flame spread on a pyrolysing area of lining. The surface temperature isotherms for the north and east wall linings when ignition occurred are shown in Figures 4 and 5. The areas bounded by the temperature isotherm lines 353°C for the north wall lining and 337°C for the east wall lining were the areas in which ignition initially occurred and this was confirmed by the observations. The differences in the shapes of the two ignition areas can be attributed to the entrainment processes which characterize this particular experiment.

Figures 6 and 7 show the surface temperature profiles measured along the central axis of the corner fire plume for the north and east wall linings respectively. The temperature profiles for locations N2 and E2 respectively correspond to the initial ignition area for the north and east wall linings. A sharp increase in

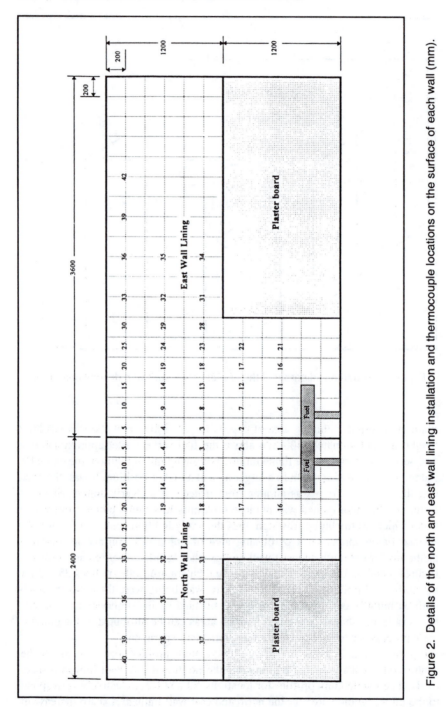

Figure 2. Details of the north and east wall lining installation and thermocouple locations on the surface of each wall (mm).

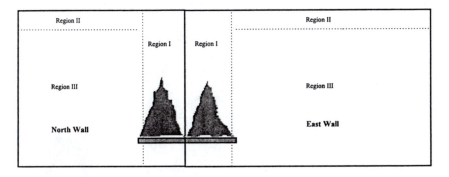

Figure 3. Schematic description of the three distinct regions of behavior for each wall.

temperatures at approximately 350°C, which may be the ignition temperature for a plywood wall lining during an enclosure fire was noted. The fall in the surface temperature profiles at locations N2, N3, and E2 before the occurrence of ignition was due to the significant heat absorption required for the pyrolysis reaction which occurred over a relatively large area. At other locations, as shown in Figures 6 and 7, sharp increases in surface temperature occurred at much lower temperatures, i.e., the surfaces were subjected to a longer preheating time for these particular locations. The precise mechanisms associated with this observed behavior are not as yet clear and require further study.

The second ignition region is an area at the interface of the ceiling and walls. It was observed that the impinging flame front swept across this region with an increasing frequency, in addition to the preheating of the lining surface by convective heat transfer of hot gas. Although the preheating increased the surface temperature of the lining, ignition did not occur until the lateral advancing flame front arrived indicating that the condition for spontaneous ignition had not occurred. The area over which ignition occurred was much smaller compared to the similar areas in region I.

As shown in Figure 3, region III is the area below the second region and adjacent to the first region. In region III, ignition was caused by the downward advancing surface flame front. Sustained ignition in this region only occurred after regions I and II had both fully ignited and a flame advanced from region II. By contrast, region I had virtually no direct influence on the occurrence of ignition in region III.

Clearly, for a given fire scenario, the ignition behaviors of plywood linings in an enclosure will vary with their locations. The area of each region may vary with fuel sizes and fire load of combustible linings but the relative positions of these regions may not. The results show that occurrence of ignition on the plywood lining surface in region I was mainly induced by the source fire plume in the

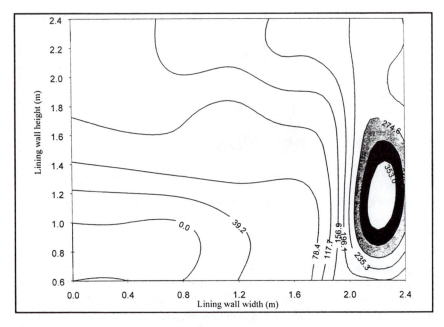

Figure 4. Isothermal profiles for the north wall lining surface at ignition (at 190 seconds).

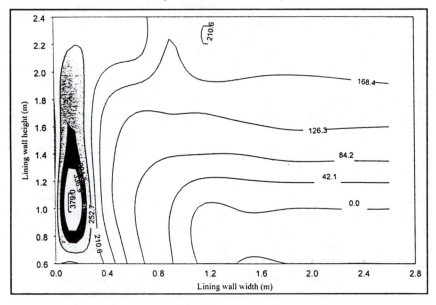

Figure 5. Isothermal profiles for the east wall lining surface at ignition (at 190 seconds).

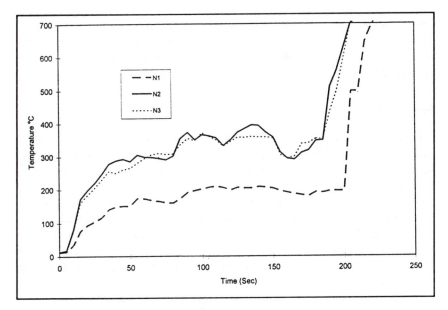

Figure 6. Surface temperature profiles for locations N1, N2, and N3 on the north wall lining.

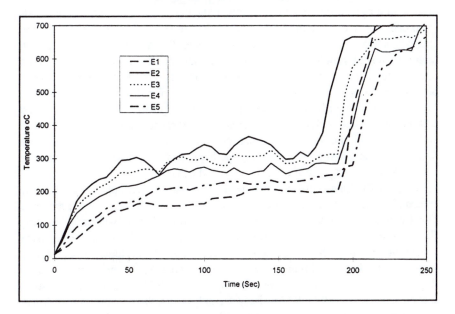

Figure 7. Surface temperature profiles for locations E1, E2, E3, E4, and E5 on the east wall lining.

corner and in regions II and III by the advancing flame front on the surfaces. Thus, the direction of the advancing flame front is directly responsible for the area of lining with the highest propensity to ignite and the ease with which ignition will occur.

Flame Spread

Flame spread behavior of the plywood linings was also different in the three regions identified with respect to ignition. Basically, region I was characterized by upward flame spread, region II by lateral flame spread, and region III by downward flame spread. In region I, upward spread of flame developed rapidly as indicated by the surface temperature profiles shown in Figure 7. Assuming ignition temperature of 350°C for the plywood linings, a rate of flame spread of 0.048 m sec^{-1} from the initial ignition area to the ceiling (from locations E2 to E5) was derived from Figure 7. This rapid flame spread is associated with a large ignition area caused by direct exposure to the fire plume in which radiation heat transfer was dominant.

In region II, flame spread laterally from the corner fire toward the door fire at the interface of the ceiling and wall linings. This area was preheated by a rapidly moving turbulent rotating flame front in which a fire ball and flame shedding was observed. When the advancing flame front approached an unburnt area of plywood lining, ignition occurred rapidly, inducing spread of flame. The preheating process increased the interior temperature of the lining and hence reduced the energy needed to cause ignition on the surface. The advancing flame front in region II moved slowly when only the east wall was lined with plywood and a rate of lateral flame spread of 0.018 m sec^{-1} was derived from Figure 8. When both the north and east walls were lined with plywood the lateral flame spread was much more rapid and a rate of lateral flame spread of 0.063 m sec^{-1} and 0.080 m sec^{-1} were derived from Figures 9 and 10 respectively for the north wall and east wall. It should be noted that the lateral flame spread from region I to region III was negligible, indicating perhaps that the flow field within the enclosure may strongly influence flame spread behavior.

In region III, flame spread was typically downward, i.e., opposed flow flame spread characterized by steadily descending linear flame front. Flame spread was directly induced by ignition of a linear region in front of the downward advancing flame front. Initially, the downward flame spread was slower than the flame spread in the other two regions but as the upper layer temperature rapidly increased, the downward flame spread rate also increased. As shown in Figure 11, the pyrolysis front moved downward from N33 to N31 in approximately fifty seconds and from N39 to N37 in forty seconds. Thus, the average rate of downward flame spread was approximately 0.018 m sec^{-1} for the north wall. As shown in Figure 12 for the east wall, the downward flame spread took approximately sixty seconds from E25 to E23 and fifty seconds from E36 to E34, resulting in an

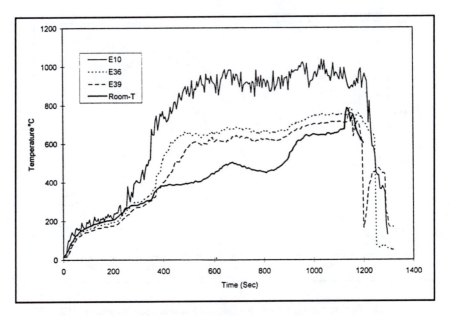

Figure 8. Surface temperature profiles for the interface locations E10,
E36, and E39 on east wall lining and enclosure temperature at
300 mm below ceiling (one side of lining installation).

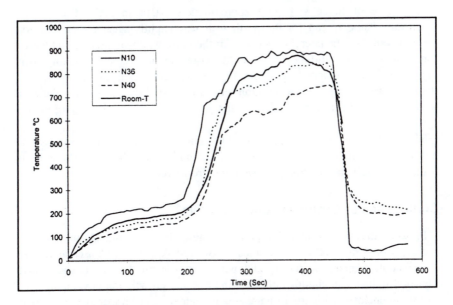

Figure 9. Surface temperature profiles for the interface locations N10, N36,
and N40 on north wall lining and enclosure temperature at
300 mm below ceiling (two sides of lining installation).

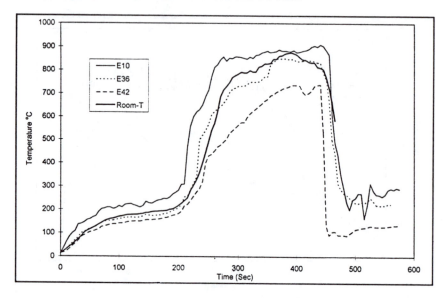

Figure 10. Surface temperature profiles for the interface locations E10, E36, and E42 on east wall lining and enclosure temperature at 300 mm below ceiling and east wall (two sides of lining installation).

average rate of flame spread of approximately 0.014 m sec^{-1}. The rate of downward flame spread for the north wall was slightly greater than that for the east wall, i.e., the lateral dimension for the north wall was smaller and therefore a more severe turbulent flow field existed in that region, resulting in a higher hot layer temperature. From Figures 11 and 12, it can be seen that the north wall lining reached ignition temperature slightly earlier than the east wall lining in the lower location of the linings within the downward flame spread region.

The results show that the flame spread behavior of plywood linings varies with not only the configuration in which it is installed but also the locations on each wall, particularly the position relative to the fire source.

Contribution of Plywood to Enclosure Fire

Plywood may be considered to be in the categories of flammable linings e.g., a class 3 or 4 material as determined in BS 476 Part 7 [6]. Consequently, its contribution to enclosure fire development is of concern. This study shows that plywood linings can significantly contribute to the growth and development of fire in an enclosure. Figure 13 compares the upper layer temperatures 300 mm below the ceiling for corner enclosure fires with and without linings installed. Clearly, without the lining, the temperature increased steadily and slowly after the

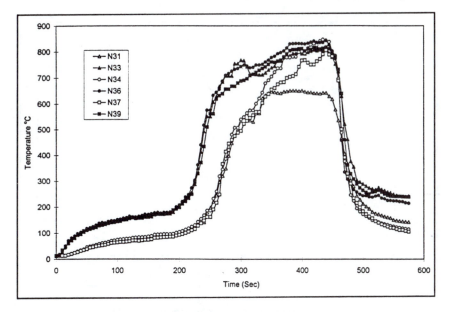

Figure 11. Surface temperature profiles at N31, N33, N34, N36, N37, and N39 on north wall lining for downward flame spread.

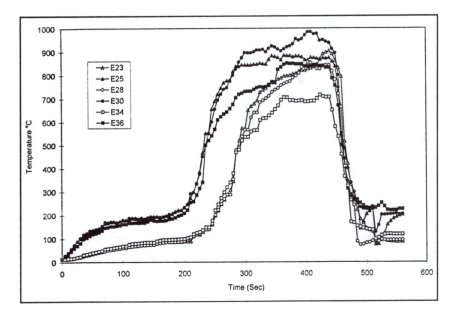

Figure 12. Surface temperature profiles at E23, E25, E28, E30, E34, and E36 on east wall lining for downward flame spread.

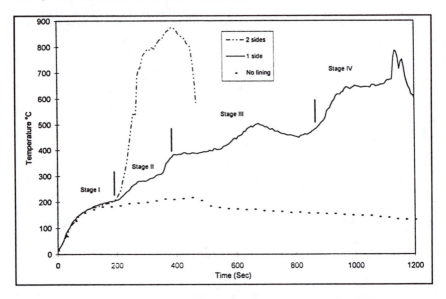

Figure 13. Comparison of upper layer temperature at 300 mm below ceiling for enclosure fires with and without plywood lining.

ignition of the fuel. By contrast, the one side lining installation (on the east wall) showed a number of temperature jump stages (see Figure 13 solid line curve) which corresponded to the flame spread behaviors exhibited principally in the three different regions. As shown in the solid line curve, stage I corresponds with the ignition of the fuel, stage II with the upward flame spread in region I, stage III with the lateral flame spread along the interface of the ceiling and the wall. Stage IV was the phase in which downward flame spread dominated. In this stage, due to the long period of preheating, the room temperature was high, the hot gas layer rapidly descended, and, therefore, the surface temperature increased rapidly. Consequently, this stage was shorter and progress toward flashover was rapid. For the two sided lining installation, the contribution of the lining to the enclosure fire was so significant as shown from the dash dot line curve in Figure 13 that fire growth was in fact dominated by the burning linings. The distinct temperature jump stages were not easily apparent because the room temperature increased so rapidly that the rise from 300°C to 600°C took only thirty seconds. By comparing room temperatures, it is clear that the plywood linings severely affect the growth of enclosure fires at various stages.

It has been shown that the plywood lining can contribute to the growth of an enclosure fire not only by extending the burning area but also by the feedback of thermal energy which accelerates the burning of the initial fuel package. In Figure 14, this is verified since the mass loss results for the fuel with and without

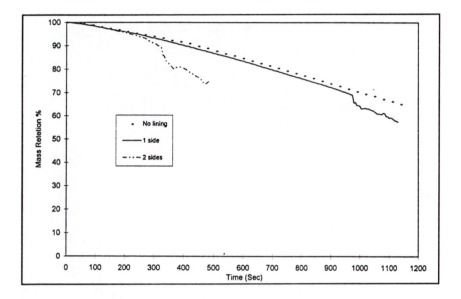

Figure 14. Comparison of fuel mass loss with and without
plywood linings during enclosure fires.

the lining installed clearly show the effect of feedback due to the lining. As
shown in Figure 14, the fuel mass loss suffered a slow steady decrease when
the lining was not installed. However, in the case of the one side lining installation, a sharp mass loss occurred at the time, which corresponds to the downward
flame spread stage which was close to onset of flashover. Similarly, in the case
of the two side lining installation, a sharp mass loss occurs but much earlier,
which corresponds to the rapid room temperature increase. In this case, over
10 percent of the mass of fuel was consumed to produce significant heat energy in
less than fifty seconds as shown from the dash dot line curve for the two sides
lining installation. Clearly, the heat feedback effect from plywood linings is
significant in enclosure fires.

Charring

Char depth data for the plywood were collected when the fire was extinguished
after flashover. The char depths were obtained by measuring the charred layer of
burnt plywood lining through various holes which were drilled in the lining
sheets. The data were then mapped utilizing contour graphs as shown in Figures
15 and 16, respectively, for the north and east walls. The results indicate that the
areas of deepest char formation are located at two distinct sections on each wall—

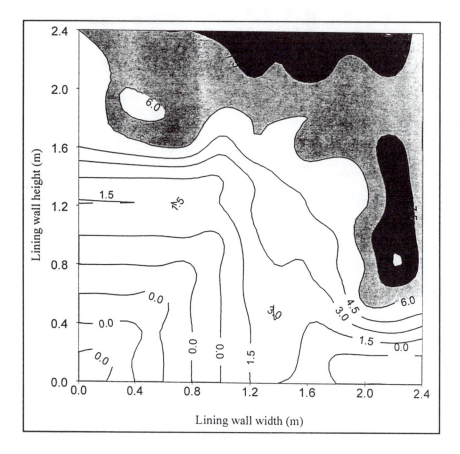

Figure 15. Profiles of equal char depths for north wall lining (mm).

one located in the area directly facing and in line with the source fire plume and the other in a strip area at the wall and ceiling interface at a small distance from the corner position. It would seem that the former area of charring was caused by the radiation from the source fire plume while the latter was more likely caused by convective heat transfer.

The char patterns also show that, for the plywood lining, there were two main surface fire sources on each wall by which the surface flame was accelerated. In particular, the local surface fire in the upper area must act as an important heat and ignition source which assists the promotion of spreading surface flame from the corner toward the door area along the interface of the ceiling and walls in region II.

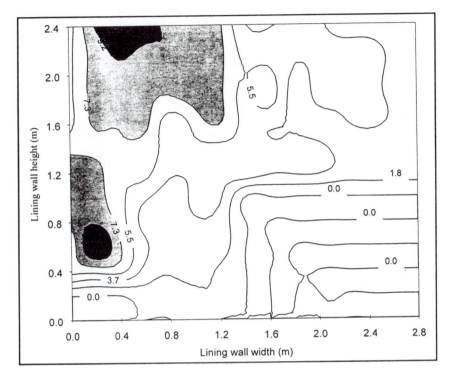

Figure 16. Profiles of equal char depths for east wall lining (mm).

SUMMARY AND CONCLUSIONS

Behavior of plywood lining in an enclosure fire, in terms of ignition, flame spread, charring, and contribution to the enclosure fire growth, was analyzed based on experimental results. When subjected to the corner fire, the adjacent walls behaved differently in the three different regions. In region I, ignition occurred in a relatively large area and flame spread rapidly. However, in region II ignition occurred in a smaller area and, also, flame spread was initially relatively slower but the rate of surface flame spread increased rapidly when enclosure temperature rose rapidly. In region III linear ignition area and a linear downward flame spread front occurred. The contribution of plywood linings to the enclosure fire was significant and the degree of influence varied with the fire behavior of the lining in each region. In region II a critical stage occurred for both the surface flame development and fire growth in the enclosure since the surface fire was not directly extended from region I to region III but from region II to region III. The observation made of this behavior is useful since it will give further direction to smaller experimental simulations and to the development of the relevant numerical modelling of the physical processes that are responsible for flame spread and fire growth.

REFERENCES

1. B. Sundstrom, Classification of Wall and Ceiling Linings, *The Proceedings of EUROFIC Seminar*, pp. 23-36, 1991.
2. B. Karlsson, *Modeling Fire Growth on Combustible Lining Materials in Enclosures*, Report TVBB 1009, Lund University, 1992.
3. U. Wickstrom and U. Goransson, Full-Scale/Bench-Scale Correlations of Wall and Ceiling Linings, *Fire and Materials, 16*, pp. 15-22, 1992.
4. N. A. Dembsey and R. B. Williamson, The Effect of Ignition Source Exposure and Specimen Configuration on the Fire Growth Characteristics of a Combustible Interior Finish Material, *Fire Safety Journal, 21*, pp. 313-330, 1993.
5. ISO 9705, *Fire Tests—Full-Scale Room Test for Surface Products*, International Standards Organisation (ISO), Geneva, 1993.
6. BS 476 Part 7, *Fire Tests on Building Materials and Structures—Method for Classification of the Surface of Flame of Products*, British Standards Institution, London, 1989.

Contributors

ALI, FARIS A., graduated with a first class Civil Engineering degree at the University of Technology, Iraq, in 1983. After three years of working as a structural engineer in Iraq where he was involved in the structural design of several projects in Baghdad, he started his postgraduate study of structural engineering in the former Soviet Union obtaining his MSc in 1988 and Ph.D. in Moscow, 1992. In the same year he arrived in the United Kingdom and worked on the performance of steel reinforced concrete structures in fire for nine years. Initially he worked as a visiting lecturer at City University (London), and currently he works as a Research Officer at the Fire Research Center, University of Ulster, UK. Research interests are: creep of concrete, thin-walled steel structures, behavior of steel columns in fire, spalling of high strength concrete under high temperatures, and performance of axially and rotationally restrained steel frames in fire.

AZHAKESAN, M. A., is a fire researcher at the University of Ulster, Fire SERT Centre, Northern Ireland.

BELLES, DONALD W., is a Senior Principal and manages the Tennessee office for Koffel Associates, Inc. Mr. Belles is a Fellow in the Society of Fire Protection Engineers, is a registered Professional Engineer and specializes in the application of fire and building codes. He is active in the development of nationally recognized Model Building and Fire Codes and currently serves as consultant to a number of large industrial organizations including the Glazing Industry Code Committee. In addition to his work with building codes, he is active within the standards developing agencies of the United States. He served on the National Fire Protection Association's Standards Council and is currently active in three of NFPA's Technical Committees responsible for maintaining building code reference standards. He is the author of a large number of articles dealing with fire safety, including sections of the NFPA Fire Protection and Life Safety Code Handbooks pertaining to egress design, fire safety in health care facilities, and other fire protection issues.

CONNOLLY, R., is at the City University, School of Engineering, Northhampton Square London, EC1V 0HB.

FLETCHER, DAVID F., received the Ph.D. degree from Exeter University in the United Kingdom in 1982. His current position is Senior Research Fellow, Department of Chemical Engineering, University of Sydney, Australia. His research interests include fire and explosions, combustion, and computational fluid mechanics.

HASSANI, S. K. S., received the Ph.D. degree from Queen's University Belfast in Northern Ireland. He served as Research Fellow at the Fire SERT Centre, University of Ulster. His primary interests in fire safety engineering include the behavior of glazing in enclosure fires and fire dynamics in room fires.

KENT, J. H., has a Ph.D. from the University of Sydney, Australia. His research interests are combustion and computational fluid dynamics.

LO, S. M., received his Ph.D. degree in Architecture from the University of Hong Kong. He is now Associate Professor in the Department of Building & Construction, City University of Hong Kong. Prior to joining City University he served for over 12 years with the Buildings Department of the Hong Kong Government where he was involved in the drafting of legislation and codes of practice. Dr. Lo also served as Secretary for the Working Party on the Review of Means of Escape Code and as member of the Working Group on Fire Safety Engineering Approach, Hong Kong Government. He has served as project leader on various building projects and as expert advisor in court cases. His research interests include fire safety and engineering, evacuation modeling, fire risk analysis, human behavior and fire and smoke modeling.

MOGHTADERI, BEHDAD, has a Ph.D. from the University of Australia. He is currently Assistant Professor (Lecturer) in the Department of Chemical Engineering at the University of Newcastle, Australia. His current research interests are combustion of solid fuels, fire safety science, computational fluid dynamics, mathematical modeling, and kinetic analysis of chemical processes.

NOVOZHILOV, VASILY, received his Ph.D. from the University of Moscow, Russia in 1993 and continued in post-doctoral studies at the University of Sydney, Australia. His current position is Assistant Professor in the Department of Mechanical Engineering at Nanyang University, Singapore. Research interests include combustion, fire safety, and computational fluid dynamics.

SHIELDS, T. JIM, is a graduate of Edinburgh University and the University of Ulster and is a Professor of Fire Safety Engineering at University of Ulster. He is Director of the Fire SERT Centre and has been involved in teaching and conducting research in Fire Safety Engineering for over twenty-five years. He is coordinator of Unit of Assessment 33 Built Environment which achieved a rating of 4 in the 1992 and 1996 research assessment exercises. His current research interests are extensive including the behavior of materials, components, and people in fire. With colleagues at Fire SERT he organized and hosted the first international symposium on human behavior in fire in September 1998. He was awarded the Association of Building Engineers "Man of the Year" award in 1995 for his work in fire safety engineering. On the international scene he has contributed to the work of the ISO the Conseil du Batiment CW14 Fire Safety Engineering, World Health Organisation and the International Association for Fire Safety Science. He was a Visitor to BRE Fire Research Station, and has contributed to the work of BSI committees in Fire Safety Engineering. Jim was appointed as a member of the Fire Authority for N.I. which is responsible for the provision of fire services in Northern Ireland.

SILCOCK, GORDON, W. H. is a Senior Lecturer in Fire Safety Engineering. He is a chartered Physicist and graduate of the Queens University of Belfast where he studied physics and mathematics. Having been involved initially in education he has for the last eighteen years been actively involved in Fire Safety Engineering Research and Education at University of Ulster.

SULLIVAN, PATRICK J. E., is a chartered civil and structural engineer and is the Principal of Sullivan & Associates, consultants in Material & Structural Investigations and Forensic Engineering since 1974. Dr. Sullivan has been a Visiting Professor and Senior Research Fellow, City University, London since 1991. Prior to this date, he was on the teaching and research staff in Concrete Technology at Imperial College of Science and Technology. He was a Specialist Quality Assessor for Higher Education Funding Council for England between 1996-98. He is currently a member/fellow of the Chamber of Architects and Civil Engineers (A. & C. E.), the Institute of Civil Engineers, Institution of Structural Engineers, the Societe des Ingenieurs et Scientifique de France, the Chartered Institute of Arbitrators London and the American Concrete Institute. He is also a member on a number of technical committees in the U.K., Europe, and the United States. Before starting his academic and research career, he was employed with Structural and Civil Engineering Consultants and Contractors over a period of ten years and was involved in design of multi-storey structures, shell structures, and in the development, design, and construction of spherical prestressed concrete nuclear pressure vessels. He has been involved in research since 1966 on concrete at fire temperatures, under cryogenic conditions, and under other extreme conditions. He has also researched on the effects of bacteria on concrete, the use of organic fibres (juncos) in concrete, the use of waste products (phosphogypsum) on concrete, and the effects of low VOC content coatings on Structural steels. Dr. Sullivan has over 70 publications in learned journals and at International

Conferences and has innumerable confidential reports for the construction industry and Government Establishments.

YEOH, G. H., obtained his Ph.D. degree in Mechanical Engineering from the University of New South Wales, Australia. He is now a Nuclear Thermal Hydraulics Professional Officer of the Australian Nuclear Science Technology Organization (ANSTO). Prior to joining ANSTO, he served for five years with the Commonwealth Scientific Industrial Research Organization (CSIRO) as a Research Scientist where he was involved in the development of analytical and numerical techniques for the evaluation of fire and smoke spread using Computational Fluid Dynamics (CFD) techniques. His research interests include fire safety and engineering, the use of CFD techniques and applications and fire, smoke, and combustion modeling.

YUEN, RICHARD K. K., obtained his Ph.D. degree in Fire Dynamics and Engineering from the University of New South Wales, Australia. He joined the Department of Building and Construction at the City University of Hong Kong in 1990. He was employed by the General Electric Company Limited (Hong Kong) and Hong Kong Electrical before taking up the lectureship in the Department of Building Services Engineering at the Hong Kong Polytechnic University. He is a registered Professional Engineer and has been engaged in consultancies for both the public and private sectors in the areas of fire safety engineering and building energy studies. His research interests include pyrolysis and combustion applications of Computational Fluid Dynamic, neural network modeling in fire engineering and HVAC systems.

ZHANG, JUN, obtained his Ph.D. at Bolton Institute U.K. in 1992 and specialized in combustion of polymeric materials and fire resistance. Since 1993 he has worked at the Fire SERT Center, University of Ulster, Northern Ireland, and now holds the position of university research fellow. His research interests include fire dynamics, compartment fires, combustion of polymeric materials, and fire resistant materials. He has had numerous publications in relation to these research areas.

ABOUT THE EDITOR

Paul R. DeCicco is Professor Emeritus at the Polytechnic University (New York) where he taught courses in Civil and Fire Protection Engineering and has served as Director of the Center for Fire Research. As principal Investigator in a wide range of fire research projects he has directed full scale fire tests for the New York Fire and Building Departments in connection with the development of building and fire codes. He has also been engaged in mathematical and physical modeling of fire phenomena in various building occupancies, and in the study of fires in large spaces. He is a fellow of the American Society of Civil Engineers and the Society of Fire Protection Engineers and currently serves as Executive Editor of the *Journal of Applied Fire Science.* Professor DeCicco is a registered Professional Engineer and has practiced Civil and Fire Protection Engineering for over forty years. He is co-author of *Making Buildings Safer for People* (Van Nostrand, 1990), and has published a number of papers on fire protection engineering. He has been honored for his research work in fire protection of high-rise buildings and in the improvement of fire safety in high risk urban residential buildings. He is currently engaged as a consultant in the investigation of fires and occasionally serves as an expert witness in fire litigations.

Index